LOSING OUR ELECTIONS

realclearpublishing.com

Losing Our Elections: What I Learned Running for Congress, and How We Can Fix Our Broken Politics

For more information, please contact:
Amplify Publishing, an imprint of Amplify Publishing Group
620 Herndon Parkway, Suite 320
Herndon, VA 20170
info@amplifypublishing.com

Library of Congress Control Number: 2022906133

CPSIA Code: PRV0622A

ISBN-13: 978-1-63755-236-0

Printed in the United States

To my wife, Tricia, for her amazing encouragement and support.

Losing
OUR
Elections

What I Learned
Running for Congress,
and How We Can Fix
Our Broken Politics

JIM SPURLINO

RealClear
Publishing

CONTENTS

Preface

LIKE MANY AMERICANS, I HAVE been a longtime observer of national politics with a deep interest in how policies can change the trajectory of our nation and the lives of our citizens. A few years ago, I decided to do something more than observe.

In 2016, I ran for an open seat in the U.S. House of Representatives. I lost. I didn't lose in the general election. I lost in the Republican primary. I finished fourth, receiving only 7 percent of the vote. That's not the typical profile of someone who writes a book about politics.

But I saw a lot, and learned even more, during my campaign, which was the first time I ran for office. This book brings together my observations and lessons learned to provide a window into how campaigns are run in the United States. You'll see the good, the bad—and yes—the ugly.

I wrote this book because I wanted to convey the inner workings of today's elections and capture what life is like on the campaign trail. I share details on how campaigns are run and what goes into a campaign. The plausible and implausible are also included. However, the "why" is here too: why people run and why they get elected. This is just as interesting and just as important. Some may find the answers intriguing, and others may just shake their heads in disbelief. Others may have their worst fears confirmed about the state of campaigns in our country.

I tried to run a campaign that would show how people from outside the political establishment could bring fresh thinking to our political debate, while also elevating the political discourse—focusing on facts and evidence as opposed to just polarizing rhetoric. While I think I mostly succeeded on both of these fronts, these contributions aren't what win elections—at least not these days. And as I explain later, there's a lot of pressure for candidates to resort to hard-edged rhetoric and hardball tactics.

I also wove into the story some of my thoughts on the shortcomings of our campaigns (and the broader political system) and what the repairs could look like. This material touches on gerrymandering, voter turnout rates, campaign finance, primaries, and voting mechanics. Even if all of my ideas were implemented, I don't think it would have changed the outcome of my race. The winner, Warren Davidson, won fair and square. But seeing how the campaign unfolded and reflecting on it afterwards led me to believe that there's a clear need for reform. As the journalist Michael Kinsley wrote many years ago: "The scandal isn't what's illegal, the scandal is what's legal."

Alongside the serious material are some stories that will surely make you smile and occasionally chuckle. It's not all bad. Many dedicated people are concerned about our country, and they take politics—and governing—seriously.

I think every American wants to see the United States succeed and wants our citizens to be prosperous. You can define national success and citizen prosperity in myriad ways, but we are on the same page when it comes to the overarching goal. We all see it when our country is under a significant threat, such as the 9/11 tragedy. Suddenly, we came together under the same patriotic banner, and we were all Americans, on the same team with no enemies within our borders. We can get back there without a national emergency. We can replace our current splintered politics and citizenry with a focus on being one nation, united. Rekindling the patriotic spirit is the great challenge before us.

Half of the work to be done is structural. This is described in the Afterword, with recommendations for modifying our election system and how the U.S. House and Senate operate. While some of the ideas may seem unorthodox and would require some rethinking about how to elect public officials, I also believe these ideas would pass muster with the Founding Fathers.

The other half of the work is a little tougher. It has to do with you. If you agree with the need for greater unity, we are most of the way there already. The last step is simply to recognize that there will be competing ideas about how to achieve this unity and to be able to *disagree* without being *disagreeable*.

President Dwight D. Eisenhower made two of my favorite statements on this topic:

- "Never question another man's motive. His wisdom, yes, but not his motives."
- "I don't think the United States needs superpatriots. We need patriotism, honestly practiced by all of us, and we don't need these people that are more patriotic than you or anyone else."

That's the same Eisenhower who was the Supreme Allied Commander in charge of all forces on D-Day. And that's the day he and the U.S. Armed Forces, along with the Allies, likely saved our country and preserved our freedom.

If we all thought more like Ike and cared less about what social media or biased reporters tell us, we would be well along toward achieving greater national unity. If we stop tearing down and attempting to destroy anyone who doesn't agree with our opinion, then we have a chance. If we give competing opinions a fair hearing and can respectfully disagree, then we have a chance.

This book is for all the citizens who can see the possibility of a brighter future for our political system. Political progress will be a big step toward getting our country to reach its full potential as well. Good luck to us all, and God bless.

INTRODUCTION

My Life Changes

AT 9:20 A.M. ON SEPTEMBER 24, 2015, a series of events unfolded, the effects of which would change my life forever. That morning Pope Francis became the first pope to address a joint session of Congress. He was there at the invitation of John Boehner, speaker of the U.S. House of Representatives and second in line of succession to the most powerful position in the world, and the House Minority Leader Nancy Pelosi. I didn't know how much my life was going to change at the time. I didn't even know why. Until the next day.

My religious faith is strong and important to me, but I'm not Catholic. And although I liked this new pope and followed his visit to the United States on the news, he wasn't the reason my life changed. My life changed because the next day Boehner announced he would be resigning at the end of October, bringing to a close twenty-five years as the U.S. representative in Congress for the Eighth Congressional District in Ohio. In announcing his resignation, Boehner said, "I woke up and said my prayers as I always do, and I said, 'You know, today I'm going to do this.'" And then he resigned. After finishing with reporters, he left as he came in, singing "Zip-a-Dee-Doo-Dah." That was vintage Boehner.

I watched the news that night in hopes of learning more about why Boehner was resigning. I suspected there was something more to this sudden resignation announcement. Flipping through the channels, I caught various reporters asking him for more information regarding his decision. Question after question was met with him repeating that he had woken up and just decided to resign.

Although Boehner was a distant acquaintance, whenever I'd see him, he would act like we were good friends. I always attributed this to good coaching by his staff. I had been a modest financial supporter of his campaigns for years and played in his golf fundraisers. Sometimes I would attend breakfasts he had for supporters in his hometown area of Butler County, Ohio. These gatherings always felt like a friendly pep rally. He would regale us with stories from DC and then tell us of his plans. Later in his career, when he became House Speaker, it was a little more formal because Secret Service accompanied him, and he rode around in the requisite black Chevy Suburban with tinted windows and police escorts. Still, he was the same guy once he started talking.

The Boehner on TV that night was classic Boehner to me, which is to say he was in charge and happy in the spotlight. I had followed him and House politics long enough to know there really was more to his resignation than he let on. For several years, he had been the nominal leader of a deeply divided Republican Party. There had been unhappiness with losing the White House and a lack of progress on conservative issues. Worse yet, the Democrats were running roughshod over him. All of this caused dissatisfaction among some Republicans and contributed to the rise of a very conservative splinter movement called the Tea Party.

The Tea Party movement started in 2009 when CNBC reporter Rick Santelli called for blunting the efforts of President Barack Obama to bail out homeowners who were defaulting on their mortgages.[1] Santelli's animated delivery helped draw attention to the message, and it became a rallying cry for disgruntled citizens. Soon, there was a Tea Party caucus within the Republican Party. They boisterously supported less government, less spending, and lower taxes. This caught the eye of David and Charles Koch, billionaire brothers who support conservative causes and politicians. Through their organization, Americans for Prosperity (AFP), they began to support and advocate for these ideas and the politicians who would work to address these issues.

Boehner was blindsided by this new group and never respected them. While firmly conservative, he also recognized the value of compromise and would do so in order to get things done. But that was anathema to those in the Tea Party. Eventually, their voices grew louder and larger in number, which imperiled Boehner's ability to lead the House. When he announced his resignation, the Republican Party looked like a ship that was taking on water. While it may be true that he decided to announce his resignation just that morning, as he said over and over on TV, it was clear to me that his interest in continuing to serve as Speaker had likely been diminishing for several months, if not years. I was surprised by his decision, but I could understand why he made it.

His resignation triggered an election to replace him. With no incumbent, and no one else with high name recognition, the Republican primary was a free-for-all. Almost immediately, several career politicians announced they would be seeking his seat. All were well liked, with conservative leanings that would be perfect for the Eighth Congressional District, which was drawn to ensure that a Republican would win every general election.

I watched these usual suspects line up for Boehner's seat with detached interest. Two held statewide office and one was a county official. I didn't think any of them would make a difference in Washington. I hoped for an outsider to emerge—someone with strong character and the brains to make a difference. Someone not addicted to getting elected term after term without contributing anything to the country. As the pool of likely successors included many of the same stale politicians, I began to think I was hoping for a miracle.

CHAPTER 1

Going to School, Getting to Work, and Catching the Political Bug

I WAS BORN AND RAISED in Dayton, Ohio, and grew up in an upper-middle-class suburban neighborhood. My parents attended the same grade school, middle school, and high school as I did. They both graduated from Northwestern University—Mom with an English degree and Dad with an engineering degree and MBA. I had two older brothers and two younger sisters, and many aunts, uncles, and cousins were around when we were young. It was a pretty nice childhood, and we were fortunate for all we had, although as a kid it didn't register how lucky we were.

There was an unspoken understanding that we were all expected to attend college. I was not a motivated student in high school and graduated in the lower third of my class. When I started college, it was more of the same for the first quarter . . . and then I dropped out. I wasn't unhappy or struggling with classes. I think I was just a little disappointed that all the classes seemed the same, and I also thought I already knew enough to conquer the world. *Ah, to be young and dumb and not know it!*

My dad told me that if I wasn't pursuing a college degree then I was going to work. So off to work I went. I got a job running a jackhammer for a highway construction company. It was hard work, but I made about fourteen dollars an hour, which was good money for the early eighties. The guys I worked with were all hard-scrabble types who lived paycheck to paycheck. I liked them a lot for their grit and toughness. Most were married and had kids, and those who didn't drove the nicer cars and pickups. Looking back, I learned a lot from them and wasn't unhappy about my choice to work instead of going back to school.

But that feeling only lasted about a year, and I started to figure out that as much as I liked the job and pay, I wasn't really going anywhere careerwise. Most of my friends were in college, and I felt like I was falling behind them. But I wasn't quite able to give up the money and the independence that came with it, so I did what seemed natural: I went back to school at the University of Dayton and kept my job. It was a juggling act at times, especially when exams rolled around, but I managed and felt good about what I was accomplishing. I also switched jobs and began working at a company that had room for me to grow. It felt like a good fit all the way around.

After four years of this, I graduated with a bachelor of science in business management. I had also worked my way up a bit at my employer and was now running a major division of this regional company. I was accustomed to the dual work and school load, and

I liked being busy, so I enrolled in my school's MBA program and started within weeks of completing my undergraduate degree. I finished my MBA coursework in two years—my GPA was just shy of a 4.0, which was at least partly a product of my paying the tuition bills and wanting to maximize the experience. Within two years of earning my MBA, I was promoted to general manager at my employer. This company was just the right fit for me at the time: they had just around one hundred employees and had a solid team of managers to work with.

After fourteen years of employment with this company, I got the itch to do my own thing. I tried buying out the owner, but he wasn't interested, so I quit and started my own company. It was 2000 and the economy was still feeling strong and banks were loaning money. With a big loan, the right people, and a little luck, I started Spurlino Materials from scratch and eventually grew it to a nationally recognized leader in the construction materials industry. In 2017, I had the good fortune of being extended an offer for my company that I couldn't refuse, so I sold it. Some of my experiences and exploits can be found in my earlier book, *Business Bullseye: Take Dead Aim and Achieve Great Success*. It includes some sound business advice as well as entertaining tales from my business career.

Growing up, my family wasn't particularly involved in politics, nor did we talk much about it much at home. I remember my parents commenting from time to time about things—maybe about a particular president or current event—but I don't remember any politically active or engaged presence in our house. I'm not totally sure what political party my parents affiliated themselves with early on. It seemed like maybe Mom was more conservative and Dad was more liberal, but there was never much discussion either way. Later in life, I definitely felt like Mom was a Republican and Dad became an Independent. My brothers and sisters seemed to sway to the left as they moved through adulthood, but I'm not totally sure of that even today.

Around the time I started college, I became more interested in current events and politics. My interest was sparked in part by Ronald Reagan's election as president. I became the nerdy twentysomething who watched the evening news and Sunday political shows. I wasn't leaning hard one way or the other, but I was absorbing a lot. As I became better informed, I felt myself leaning to the right more and more and identifying as a Republican. The times may have had something to do with it. While I thought Reagan was a lot like an old movie actor (which, of course, he was), I found myself agreeing with his principles, ideas, and strategies. I was also impressed by his results, which included a robust economy and our country's standing in the world taking on unprecedented importance. This was quite a contrast to the Jimmy Carter years.

As much as I was absorbing and staying current with political events, I didn't become one of those people at parties who goes on and on about their political views. In fact, I was the last person to bring up political topics in conversation. It's not that I didn't feel strongly about my views—I just wasn't interested in participating in what I thought were just opinionated diatribes without any real discussion of merit. However, when political topics did come up, I wasn't shy about the facts. I embodied the phrase, "Everyone is entitled to his own opinion but not his own facts." I wouldn't let people get away with sharing incorrect information, but I wasn't interested in debating opinions either.

As I grew older, I became more interested in political ideas and what needs could be met through a mix of good governing and smart public policy, more so than just keeping tabs on current events. It was more about becoming a stronger country: more secure, more prosperous, and creating more opportunities for all (including my old jackhammer buddies). I also had a greater appreciation for my own good fortune in being born into a family with resources to buy a nice home, eat good food, drive nice cars, and attend good schools. This reflection and appreciation made me think more about those less fortunate and the best way to lift all boats with a rising tide rather than just my own ship's condition.

While my thinking evolved, it never drove me to seek any kind of elected office. I never ran for anything—not even student council. I was content with seeking knowledge and then applying it by helping others get elected. I was passionate about issues facing the federal government, but I was much less interested in state and local issues. While I was not a great student in high school, I became engrossed in U.S. history and read extensively about our country's founding, the Founding Fathers, and many great leaders throughout time.

This passion led to many spirited discussions with friends, colleagues, and the occasional politician. Over time, I evolved from being an interested political observer to someone who would engage in debates of current issues, earnestly looking for real solutions to make our country a better place. I also became more active in pressing elected officials for change where I saw opportunity to make our government more effective and fiscally responsible. Initially, this was in matters that affected my company and industry as well as matters pertaining to early childhood, where I had a passion to help at-risk families with young children. Later, this expanded to many other topics and issues as my interests and concerns expanded. But never in my wildest dreams did I think I would run for Congress.

CHAPTER 2

Deciding to Run

NEARLY TWO MONTHS HAD PASSED since Boehner announced his resignation, and none of the announced candidates for his seat seemed up to the standards I had hoped for. I wasn't so much looking for a Boehner-like person as much as someone who wasn't just running because they saw Congress as the logical next step in their political career.

Ohio had passed term limits for most state offices in 1992. Since then, most offices were limited to two four-year terms, and state representatives were limited to four two-year terms. At the time, this seemed to appeal to many as a way of limiting how long someone could serve in a single position. Many Republicans—particularly conservative Republicans—felt term limits would put a stop to career politicians who often become more liberal while in office.

However, the intended purpose for the term limits wasn't necessarily realized. It ended up encouraging a sort of seat swapping.

Many state representatives would simply serve the maximum number of terms and then shift to a Senate seat, where there were regular openings. After maxing out in the state senate, they would hope to run for a statewide office, like secretary of state or attorney general, and then on to lieutenant governor or governor. Along the way, they might get a shot at a U.S. representative opening.

In other words, term limits really didn't work out the way many voters had hoped. It was all too often and all to obvious that party leaders and influencers made sure there was a path to continue in policymaking. This was bothersome to me but not the end of the world. It helped end the careers of some lifelong politicians, but it also contributed to several career politicians lining up to run for Boehner's seat.

Seeing this made me roll my eyes and get this "here we go again" feeling. Essentially, it was business as usual with a state representative and state senator from Boehner's district immediately lining up to run, along with the local auditor from Boehner's home county. Of course, there were a few others who got in early too, but no one recognizable nor anyone with a decent resume.

Initially, I didn't tell anyone that I was thinking of entering the race, not even my wife. I felt it was just passing curiosity and kind of "what if" thoughts while driving to work or an appointment. As time went on, I looked closer at the announced candidates and became a little more vocal to friends about my disappointment in who was running. I saw these candidates as mostly politicians with no meaningful accomplishments in office. I was hoping to see new blood who had real-world experience (ideally in the private sector). That got me thinking that *I* fit the profile of what I wanted to see in a candidate. When I expressed my disappointment about the announced slate of candidates, I would often get asked what type of person should run and then, of course, those close to me asked: "Why don't you run?"

I started many of these conversations. Maybe I was looking for validation, but in the back of my mind I was gauging the thoughts of others and seeing if the same suggestion might come unsolicited again. *"Why don't you run?"* Finally, after hearing it several times from people I trust, I broached the subject with my wife.

Tricia and I had been married several years, and it was the third marriage for both of us. We are deeply connected and feel like we've been together forever. She is truly my soul mate. I trust her completely and knew she would give the straight scoop on her thoughts. I sat down with her one night and reviewed the Boehner situation, focusing on the candidates vying for his seat. I also talked about why I wanted to run as well as the profile of who I thought would be the right candidate.

I didn't like that many of the candidates were career politicians, going from one office to the next, jockeying for the next bigger job. And they undoubtedly saw Congress as the ultimate lifetime position, getting reelected time and again regardless of their performance.

I thought I could make a difference doing what I always did in every job I ever had: Show up early and work late. Know the issues inside and out. Know the point of view of my peers and my opponents and know how to make progress when we don't agree.

I believed that the traits that made me a good businessman and community leader would also make me a good congressman. I was educated both formally and in the school of hard work. I had the skills to lead management teams as well as teams working hourly labor jobs. I spent significant time in business understanding government ways and means as well as significant time advocating for good policies that benefit families facing adversity. I had experience working with Republicans and Democrats in my advocacy efforts and always found common ground. I knew what it took to earn trust and value that trust as I worked for the common good, whether in my business for me and all my employees or in the community for the good of all. I was thoughtful, reasonable, and caring while being principled and true to myself and others whom I was responsible for.

I also thought I could make a difference in our federal government, which I believed had grown bloated and inefficient. There were too many regulations that didn't make sense and strangled business growth and investment. Federal agencies were increasingly doing a lousy job when private enterprise could do better with less funding.

Several other issues interested me, including national security, intelligence, immigration, taxes, the size of government, autonomy for the states, and helping the disadvantaged move out of poverty. As I explained my thought process, Tricia was patient and listened intently. Finally, I got to the part where others had asked about me running, and I asked her, "Do you think I should consider it?" There was no hesitation. She emphatically said "Yes!" and then launched into why I would be a great congressman. After getting my ego back in check, we talked more about what it would mean. Campaigning, people saying mean things, the impact on our eight kids, spending so much time in DC, etc. None of this changed her mind or even had her hesitating.

It was pretty exhilarating to have that conversation, and it was what I needed to get me over the hump of truly thinking about running. I told her we should both think about it and talk more in the coming days. I wasn't ready to commit to the race, but it gave me the green light to think about it in real terms, because without Tricia's approval, I would have laid it all to rest and not given it another thought.

Over the following two weeks, now in early November, any time I wasn't engaged in my business I couldn't help but think about the possibility of running. And even while working, I was often thinking about a potential campaign. It seemed like at least once or twice a day I would leave my office and drive around aimlessly as I considered the prospect of running for Congress, and just as often, the prospect of being a U.S. congressman.

My position and responsibilities as CEO of my company kept me from making the decision to run immediately. There were many factors and impacts to consider that would follow a decision to run. We had manufacturing plants in Ohio, Kentucky, and Indiana and nearly 200 employees. I had founded the company fifteen years earlier and was still very much a hands-on CEO. Although I had a very capable set of senior managers, I worked sixty-plus hours a week and took little time off. I liked my business, its successes, and being CEO. The autonomy and freedom it gave me was one of the ultimate rewards of my hard work.

One of the biggest hurdles in moving forward to run was scoping out what would happen to my business. While I was constantly engaged in leading the business, I knew my senior management team would be able to continue to operate it just as successfully. I considered two important factors beyond that.

First, I would have to bring in someone to be CEO if elected. While the existing management *was* very good, they would still need a single leader. I was fortunate in that I was very active in my industry and several people stood out as potential candidates to step into my shoes. After some time and a few confidential conversations with people I trusted, I became comfortable that there could be a smooth transition if I departed. I also knew that I was not disappearing to an island without communication.

Second, I explored how much the company would lose in value because of my absence. I knew I was not irreplaceable and that there were surely some potential future CEOs who would have been better than me, but I also knew that there would be an inevitable loss of value to the company. In real terms, this meant there would be opportunities missed, progress delayed, and profits forgone without me. Maybe just for a short term or maybe for longer, but replacing me as CEO—at the company I founded and had always led—with someone new would lead to loss of value. I could not be sure how much, but it was definitely a sacrifice I needed to figure into the equation of running or not.

The biggest decision I had to make was whether *I* wanted to run and whether *I* wanted to be a U.S. congressman. It was truly a blessing to have my wife's support and be able to envision my business being alright without me. But it came down to whether I wanted to do this. And why.

The most important reason for me to run was to make a difference. It was high-minded, but I firmly believed I could make a difference. I felt I could contribute to making our country better and be part of a sea change in remaking our government so it would be *for* the people. I knew I had the drive to do this, and when motivated I can work as hard as anyone. I also thought this was a unique time for me. A time when I could step away from my business and make this contribution for my country. I wanted to do it and was able. All of these were big factors in my thinking.

I also could not help but question whether there was some ego-driven part of me that wanted to run for elective office. I had seen that ego-driven side of politicians all too often and absolutely did not want that to be part of my motivation. Yes, we all seek validation and even acclaim for our accomplishments, but I kept coming back to the work to be done. I continued to hear an inner voice ask the question, *Are you going to be okay if you're elected, do great work, and receive no credit?* The answer to my own question always had a parallel. In many of my donations to charities, I usually asked that I not be known as the donor and to be listed as "anonymous." It wasn't anything but a way to keep myself in check. I always wanted to make these donations (occasionally seven figures) without being recognized for them and to make sure I was doing it for the right reasons (which have *not* been about me). I think this parallel answered my question.

The last hurdle for me was the most important one. Running for office, and putting in the hard work once you are there, is a sacrifice. I needed to make sure my wife was 100 percent in on that because she would be making just as big a sacrifice. In the final two weeks before making the decision to run, she and I talked more and more about this. She never wavered and never gave me a reason to think she was anything less than 100 percent supportive.

CHAPTER 3

Hiring My Campaign Team

I MADE THE DECISION TO run for Congress on one of my many drives away from the office to think. I had been back and forth and probably never close to 100 percent, but something clicked and I said out loud to myself, "I'm going to do it."

I got home that night and told Tricia. She was excited and proud and showed it. Her response sealed it for me. She believed in me, believed I would make a difference, and was full of energy and love for the new adventure that we were about to begin. That night, I spent hours making lists of what I thought was next, most of which was unfamiliar to me. I just knew I needed to get going with my education about the next steps.

First and foremost, I needed to find someone to help with this uncharted territory. I figured that must mean a campaign manager. The next morning, I phoned a political consultant I knew from working together on advocacy issues in Ohio. He was very well known and highly respected. We chatted for a bit and then I told him, "I don't know if I'm crazy or not, but I'm going to run for Boehner's seat." His reaction was nonchalant, almost as if he received such calls regularly. He told me that there were a few good consultants out there, and I needed to hire one right away. We talked some more, then he asked me a strange question. "There is one guy that is really good, probably the best in the state. I don't know if he's available, but I have to tell you he's kind of rough. Will pull out all the stops. The win-at-all-costs kind of guy. Would you be okay with that?" he asked.

I wasn't sure what to make of the comments or the question. My first and unspoken reaction was, "Of course, I want to win," but internally, I heard a nagging second reaction: *What's win-at-all-costs mean?* I had to know, so I asked just that. I didn't get many specifics in his answer, just more of the "he plays hardball" and other such euphemisms. I didn't give a definitive yes or no answer to the consultant's question, but I agreed that he could reach out and see if the hardball operator was available and interested. I wasn't entirely comfortable and still didn't understand what he was trying to tell me, but I figured making the call was fine. He said he'd get back to me soon.

It was late that day that he called back. Mr. Hardball was not available and was already working for another candidate in the race. I was disappointed not to get the "best" but a little relieved I wouldn't have to explore Mr. Hardball's ethics and integrity. My consultant friend had anticipated the need for a backup plan and had already contacted another consultant who was available for this race. I got his contact information and called the new consultant as soon as I hung up.

The consultant, Mark Weaver, answered the phone on the second ring, and I introduced myself. We traded some pleasantries and got right down to it. Mark probed me a bit first. He asked who I was and why I wanted to run. It felt a little like an interview, but Mark was easy to talk to and I had a good first impression of him. After telling him about myself, it was my turn to ask questions, which included asking about his experience in running campaigns. He had some good answers. Several were high profile, and he touted his high winning percentage. He immediately told me that I had a very good chance and that he liked my story. I appreciated the comments but also knew he was now trying to get hired.

We set up a time to meet at my house a few days later. I made sure Tricia was available. Around 6:30 p.m. on the agreed day, the doorbell rang and my heart started beating a little faster. The campaign for Congress was now feeling more like reality than just talk. Mark came in and we shook hands. I introduced him to Tricia and the three of us sat down at the kitchen table. The kids stayed in their rooms for the next hour and a half, so Tricia and I were alone with Mark.

Our meeting was a combination of meet and greet and a dive into the nuts and bolts of a campaign as well as expected next steps if I were to proceed. Mark was intelligent, easy to talk to, and full of facts and information. I learned a lot of interesting and new things about campaigning. Some of which included:

1. I would need to spend a lot of time on the campaign. Mark said initially about 50 percent but that it would grow to 90 percent as time went on.

2. I would need to raise a lot of money. He estimated that at least $750,000 was needed to be competitive but that more was better.

3. Much of the money was needed to build my name recognition. At the time, I was essentially a zero in name ID, which I didn't believe could be true. Mark explained that in the eyes of voters, I was starting from scratch versus the candidates who had run multiple campaigns over the years as they ran for other offices. He estimated that building my name recognition could cost $500,000 or more.

4. We would need to hire a campaign manager. Mark explained that he was considered a consultant and that while he would handle all messaging and marketing, a campaign manager was needed to attend to day-to-day activities and logistics. This was major news to me. I thought the campaign manager was in charge, but Mark made it clear this was not the case. He would still be leading the campaign, but the campaign manager was needed for what sounded like "operations." I likened it to a CEO and COO, and he agreed with the parallel.

5. Mark volunteered to draft position papers for me, covering the issues that were likely to be most important during the campaign. He felt after this one meeting that he had a sense of what my positions were and that he could also add nuances that would boost my popularity with voters. He made it clear that I could obviously reject or edit the position papers to make them all my own, but he wanted to do the first draft.

6. Mark would handle all media and advertising production and direction. This meant he would be producer, director, editor, and writer for all campaign material. He would handle this as part of his fees but also charge a percentage on top

of the expenditures. This sounded a lot like double dipping, but apparently it was the way many such "consultants" work. His base fee was $10,000/month. This would run until the campaign ended, whether that was after the Republican primary or, if I won, the general election.

Before Mark left that evening, he promised to send me a draft of his contract. He said that if I wanted to proceed, I should decide soon, since other candidates were campaigning already and there was also a filing deadline to register as a candidate in about three weeks. He also said he was going on vacation the next day and would be gone for a week. While that didn't sound ideal, he reassured us that it would not affect how quickly our campaign could get up and running.

Tricia and I thanked Mark for his time and walked him to the door. I told him I would be in touch within a week. We closed the door and just stared at each other. Then a big smile crossed Tricia's face, and she asked what I thought. I admitted that a few things surprised me but that, overall, Mark seemed very sharp and could be the right guy. Tricia doesn't care for the side of me that is careful and uses measured words. The words "seemed" and "could" were exactly that. We sat and talked for hours after that, and I had to admit that Mark was a good fit for the job, particularly given that I didn't have other options, nor the time to explore if there were any other options out there. We had less than a week to make a decision about whether to hire Mark.

A few days later, I called him to say I wanted to hire him. He seemed excited and let me know he would be back in three days and we would get started immediately. In the meantime, he would send me a questionnaire to fill out regarding my positions on key issues. That arrived later the same day via email. It was my first look at what Mark thought would be the most important issues during the campaign. I was excited to look through it and eager to start filling it out. Discussing issues and staking out positions was what I had been doing with politics for the last two decades, and I was ready to dig in.

CHAPTER 4

Positions, Politics, and People

MARK'S QUESTIONNAIRE SEEMED FAIRLY STRAIGHT-FORWARD. I liked being able to see what issues he thought were important, but I mostly liked drafting my answers. Many of the issues were ones I had spent a lot of time thinking about before meeting Mark, and others were ones that I didn't think mattered much, but I went along with answering them all.

I devoted several hours to completing the questionnaire and was eager to send Mark my answers. I looked forward to his responses and perhaps discussing how I came to adopt my views. But Mark's response was more along the lines of, "These are good answers but . . ." And what came after "but" was what *he* thought I should say about these topics. He said our answers were not that far apart, but his version would get me more votes. He was nice about it but pretty firm in his opinion. In his view, I needed to move further to the right to win the primary. Then in the general election I could pivot more toward the center. His biggest pitch to me was, "These answers will get you elected, then you can go do great things in DC. Isn't that what you want?"

His answers were consistent with what most of the district's Republicans probably wanted to hear. It was (and still is) a very Republican district—it's the most Republican in Ohio. In 2016, 65 percent of the district's voters supported Donald Trump. Four years later, he did slightly better, winning 66 percent.[2] Nearly 90 percent of the district is white, 6 percent black, 3 percent Hispanic, and less than 2 percent Asian. People are generally middle class with a median household income that in 2019 was $62,845. The high school graduation rate is 88 percent, which is higher than the state and national average, but the college graduation rate is just 21 percent.[3]

If you looked at the district lines on a map, you'd ask how anyone could ever come up with such a thing. (The district lines can be seen in the Afterword.) The answer is that the district had been drawn to be a safe Republican seat—and having an Ohio power broker like John Boehner representing it pretty much ensured the lines would be stacked in the GOP's favor. (This is known as gerrymandering; both parties do it, and I explain it in more detail in the Afterword.) The district is decidedly suburban, with the largest city (Hamilton) having a population of about 63,000. Cincinnati and Dayton are the closest big cities.

Geographically, the district borders Indiana along four of its six counties. These areas are largely agricultural. Its southern border consists of several suburban areas of Cincinnati. Folks living in these areas would largely consider themselves part of Cincinnati.

As you travel north through the district, it runs along the western border of Dayton, then takes a right turn over the top of the city and to the east where it encompasses the smallish city of Springfield. Much of the area is home to folks who work in Dayton, or as in the southern portion, consider themselves as part of Dayton.

A prominent feature of the district is its close proximity to Wright-Patterson Air Force Base (WPAFB). It is the largest single-site employer in Ohio, with over 30,000 people working there. While still an active U.S. Air Force base, its focus today is mostly on other air force programs and their management. WPAFB is said to control more Department of Defense dollars than any other facility.

The district was, of course, strongly associated with John Boehner, who was first elected to the House in 1990. He had a great personal story. He was born in a suburb of Cincinnati, one of twelve children, and started working in the family bar at age eight. He was the first in his family to earn a college degree, and he took a job in sales shortly thereafter.[4]

He always had an interest in politics and had served on a local township board of trustees and as a state representative prior to his first run for Congress. He was fairly well known locally and widely liked. His sales skills shined through when running for these early political offices. His first run for Congress came on the heels of a sex scandal that enveloped the then-incumbent Donald "Buzz" Lukens. This opening gave Boehner the opportunity he craved, and he jumped at it. Campaigning endlessly throughout a somewhat rural district, Boehner could speak comfortably with folks from almost any background. He won that first primary with 49 percent of the vote, then won the general election easily.

He hit the ground running in his first year, grabbing headlines as a member of the "Gang of Seven"—a group of freshman Republicans who publicized the House banking scandal and then the congressional post office investigation. This same group continued to garner publicity and influence for other subsequent investigations of congressional abuse. By 1994, he was clearly a rising star and contributed to the Contract with America, which was a cornerstone of the Republican takeover of the House for the first time in forty years.[5]

For the next ten years, Boehner held various positions of influence including chairman of the House Republican Conference and chairman of the House Committee on Education and Labor. He continued to enjoy popularity and influence both in DC and at home in Ohio. His reelections became routine with 30 to 45 percent margins over his Democratic opponents (including two elections in which he ran unopposed).

In 2005, Boehner won a close election to become majority leader after Tom DeLay resigned. This meant he was the second-highest-ranking member of the House Republicans, behind Speaker Dennis Hastert. Following the 2006 elections in which the Republicans lost control of the House, Boehner was elected minority leader and was the leader of his party in the House. Two elections later, he was elected Speaker, as his party took back control of the House. It was a position he treasured and held for almost five years.

My own recollections of Boehner mainly were from one of two different perspectives. The first was from a professional perspective. I would occasionally get involved in issues that were important to my industry and/or business in general. In these instances, my conversations with him were brief and unplanned (usually at an event that he attended), and he would seem interested but also anxious to move on to another topic or person. I do give him credit though for listening and hearing me because my interactions with his staff, days or weeks later, were substantive. During his tenure as Speaker, he could increase the chances of an issue I had raised with him getting noticed and making it to the House floor. I'm sure not because of me, but maybe it was because I was one of the many voices he heard.

The second perspective was from a social view. These instances would commonly come up at a Boehner event of some sort where he invited "friendlies" only or was raising money. These were fun, and you got to see Boehner being Boehner. Social, charismatic, engaging, funny, and unfiltered. I remember group breakfasts with him where he told us about DC and the good fight he was waging. I also remember golf outings where he would show up late and drink and smoke late into the night. In later years when he was Speaker, he would be a little more guarded—both verbally and by Secret Service.

While I lacked Boehner's personal skills—and didn't have any political experience—I nonetheless thought I would be a good fit for the district. I had lived in the area for my entire life and had owned or operated businesses in the district for the previous thirty years, employing about 200 people.

One of the little-known facts about members of Congress is that they're not required to live in the district they represent. I had learned this many years earlier, and it applied to me: I lived just outside the borders of the Eighth Congressional District (though my office was in the district). While I knew that could become a campaign issue, I was confident that I could overcome it, since I believed I knew the district better than any other candidate.

In fact, I would look forward to the issue being raised (and it occasionally was), because it was a chance for me to prove I was the best candidate. My answer usually went something like this:

"It is true that I don't live in the district, but Article I of the U.S. Constitution doesn't require it. In fact, our Founding Fathers wanted it this way so that the House was the least restrictive and most open to merit of the two legislative bodies. The way this district is shaped, it wraps around my home, which is a mere five minutes away from the district.

"But rather than talk about the address of where someone sleeps, let me talk about my experience with the district. For the last thirty-one years, I have spent almost all my waking hours in the district. Until 1999, I worked for a company, Moraine Materials, that had a major presence in the district, with multiple manufacturing facilities and hundreds of employees. In 2000, I started my own company, Spurlino Materials, and built our first manufacturing facility and our headquarters in the heart of the district. I chose this location because I believe in this area and wanted to remain a part of it. It's the biggest investment of my life.

"Since starting my company, we have supplied concrete on many major construction projects, including runways and buildings at Wright-Patterson Air Force Base, Dayton International Airport, AK Steel, and Interstates 70 and 75. We've participated in constructing the tallest buildings in the area and the tallest and longest bridge in Ohio, the Jeremiah Morrow Bridge. In fact, many in the district walk, ride, or drive on my concrete every day of their lives.

"In addition to my concrete, I employ about 200 people and do business with hundreds of other corporations in the district. Even if you don't walk, ride, or drive on my concrete every day, I bet you know someone who works for me or who works for another corporation we do business with. Besides business, I am an active community volunteer and support organizations that seek to help those less fortunate, while also serving on several

of their boards. This includes multiple United Ways and Every Child Succeeds, a nationally known organization where I am chair of the board that serves at-risk families with young children.

"I know this district better than any of these other candidates. I'm here all day, every day. I do business in every corner of the district, and my business and community work touch the lives of thousands and thousands of our residents. I think voters deserve the best representative in Congress, and nobody knows this district better than I do."

I ran as a conservative—an apparent prerequisite to winning the GOP primary—but one part of my political profile made me highly unorthodox among the district's Republicans: I had voted for Barack Obama when he was running for president against John McCain. (Obama received just 36.4 percent of the district's vote.[6]) It wasn't an easy decision, but I was taken by Obama's eloquence and his vision, and I thought he could reverse some of the Bush administration's aggressive policies related to Iraq and terrorism, while I feared McCain would amount to more of the same (and maybe even worse). I also thought Obama could do something about the country's racial tensions, particularly given that he was biracial.

My vote for Obama was never an issue during the campaign because no one ever asked me whom I supported in 2008—probably because no one could have imagined a Republican voting for Obama. And while I had no plans to advertise my 2008 vote (doing so would have been political suicide), I would have revealed it had I ever been asked.

In any case, I kept an open mind and read through Mark's proposed answers to the questions. Here are a few questions, with our respective answers.

Where do you stand on abortion?

JIM	MARK
I believe that (1) federally, *Roe v. Wade* will not get overturned, has been modified by other cases subsequent to it, and the SCOTUS will continue to rule on state laws that push these federal limits; and (2) states should continue to have their own say on state abortion laws, rights, and regulations. I'm personally pro-life but tolerant of any individual's own position on this. Moreover, I'm not interested in a person's position on abortion becoming a litmus test for anything. On Planned Parenthood, I don't believe any federal funding should go toward abortions, and a thorough investigation will reveal if that happened. The majority of what PP does is actually good and not related to abortions.	As a father and Christian, abortion is abhorrent to me. Life begins at conception. That's why I'm pro-life. Planned Parenthood and other abortion providers shouldn't get a nickel of taxpayer money.

Where do you stand on gay marriage?

JIM

I have friends who are gay, and many have been in long-term committed relationships. I think our country as a whole has evolved a lot in the last few years regarding this topic, and I think we all should be more receptive to allowing gay marriage. Public officials should be punished for not following the law. It's not an option for me or you, and they should not be any different. As for businesses, in general it should be the same.

I added on the topic of gay adoption: I have two adopted daughters. They are wonderful girls, and I could not imagine my world without them any more than a biological child. I also realize that a lot of "who" they are comes from their genes. I may be able to influence them, but largely they are who they are, unique, special, and in many ways unattributable to me. Many gay couples would make great parents and some may not, just as with heterosexual couples. Having gone through the screening and selection process for an adoption, I trust that adoption agencies do their best to link quality potential parents with birth parents and their child. This wouldn't change. Would you rather see a child with a gay couple that was perfectly suited for the child or a heterosexual couple that isn't?

MARK

God ordained marriage between one man and one woman. Five judges in Washington don't get to change that. I would support a constitutional amendment to allow states to decide marriage policy. The Tenth Amendment already says that, but given the Supreme Court's narrow holding, we will need a new amendment.

Where do you stand on gun laws?

JIM	MARK
I own several pistols and rifles. My wife owns a pistol. We both completed gun safety training and are current holders of concealed carry permits. I believe this is a basic right. I also think we should strengthen the gun purchase permitting process as much as possible, even though it may not be a statistically significant problem for crimes committed with guns. The gun show loopholes need to be closed. Last, unaddressed mental health problems are the real issue in gun crimes and gun violence. There needs to be significantly more resources toward this issue and legislation that addresses gun ownership in cases of mental illness.	Our God-given constitutional right to keep and bear arms must be defended. When the Founding Fathers wrote "shall not be infringed," they meant what they said. We support our police, but we know that we must be our own first responders while we wait for help from 911 to arrive. I will fight each and every attempt to erode gun rights.

What would you do to create more jobs and boost the economy in southwestern Ohio?

JIM

I'd start by addressing the burdensome regulations that affect most businesses. Many of these regulations have little value to the general population, add huge costs to businesses and their employees, and are not implemented nor enforced in a fair and consistent manner. We should start by passing the REINS Act and the SCRUB Act. (1) The REINS Act allows Congress to have oversight over executive rulemaking on legislation that has an impact of $100 million or more on the economy. This is accountability on legislation going forward. (2) The SCRUB Act identifies major rules in effect for more than fifteen years and have undue burdens on businesses. It would eliminate or modify these with a goal of reducing regulatory costs by at least 15 percent. This is accountability on prior legislation. Overall, these two pieces of legislation would reduce regulation burdens and allow businesses to expand and even flourish, benefiting the economy and its employees.

MARK

I'm worried about the Obama economy and hardworking families. Banks no longer support small businesses because of politically motivated regulations from bureaucrats and professional politicians. Working families are faced with the worst recovery in generations. I will be outspoken against wasteful spending such as the $1.7 billion the federal government spends annually on empty office buildings. I will support free-market, patient-centered reforms to health care and create landmark tax reform.

How should the U.S. government fight terror at home and abroad?

JIM	MARK
Secure our own homeland as a priority so there are no more threats of terrorism within our borders. This means better border security and improving our intelligence community's work and collaboration with military and our allies.	America must lead. Defeat ISIS and start with calling evil by its name: radical Islamic terrorism. They want to kill us, so let's kill them first. More strikes with special forces to destroy their infrastructure and oil supplies. No more Syrian refugees in the United States until we are safe at home. No more of Obama drawing lines in the sand while the rest of the world saw how weak a leader he is by not backing up his own threat.

I added more on Syria: Some facts help. Since 2010, our country has received about 20,000 applicants from Syrians asking for refugee status. On average, it takes two years to process. Of those 20,000, about 2,000 were approved, and most of these Syrians are children or parents with children. Other countries are similar. Since 9/11, we have processed over 800,000 applications from all over the world, of those 800,000, three that were let in were subsequently found to be planning terrorism acts. All three were caught before they acted. And none were Syrians.

Do you think taxes are too high, and what should we do about it?

JIM	MARK
Individual tax rates may be higher than optimal, especially for the middle class. We need to do more for those struggling in the middle and below. Lowering their tax rates and tax filing burden makes sense. The corporate side is much worse. Our corporate tax rates are *not* competitive with the world and are causing American companies to keep over $2 *trillion* overseas and consider inversions and more. We desperately need to address this by (1) making our corporate tax rates competitive with the rest of the world and (2) giving American companies with overseas dollars a way to bring them home, such as a tax holiday. The answer is not to consider ways to legislate away inversions and tax havens but to find ways to motivate companies to stay here, bring their money home to invest in America, and invite the rest of the world to join them.	Taxes are way too high. Reform the entire tax code with a flat tax that removes the need for the IRS. Federal agencies should have to prove annually that their spending won't kill American jobs or unnecessarily add to working families' tax burden.

Where do you stand on immigration?

JIM	MARK
My grandfather arrived from Italy at Ellis Island when he was nineteen years old. He complied with all the laws, entered our country, got a job, and paid taxes. He became a citizen and lived here the rest of his life. He worked for NCR and was awarded many patents for his work, all benefiting his employer and our country. I remember times when people would say to him, "You're Italian, right?" and his answer was always the same: "No, I'm an American." He was proud of that, and we should be proud of our heritage as a welcoming nation. *Illegal* immigration is a different issue. We should enforce our laws. To this end, we should never stop doing more to secure our borders and protect our country. This may include improving funding for border security, building walls, making sure businesses aren't employing illegal immigrants, and funding our law enforcement to do their job.	Illegal immigrants are taking jobs from Americans who need jobs to support their families. The flood of illegal immigrants increases the financial burden on taxpayers and in far too many cases makes our communities more dangerous. We must secure the border and aggressively enforce the current immigration laws. Employers who hire illegal immigrants should be dealt with severely, and when law enforcement encounters an illegal immigrant, that person should be deported within days.

I was never completely comfortable with Mark's answers. He continued to press me, assertively but not too aggressively, to adopt his answers or at least something close to them. He would cajole me and ask whether his answers were really that different from mine, or whether I could "live" with his version. Our discussions always came back to whether I wanted to get elected to "go do great things in DC." I wasn't being bullied and I could have just said no to some of his answers, but I was conflicted.

I found myself reasoning that his answers weren't wrong or substantively different than mine. I thought maybe it was just the way he phrased things and that other candidates do this sort of thing all the time. For instance, did I believe marriage is between one man and one woman? Yes. Did I oppose same-sex marriage? No. So can't the two positions coexist?

In the end, I let myself believe the rhetoric that I was not betraying my own positions and was simply using a more marketable, voter-friendly version of them to get through the primary. Once through the primary, I could elaborate on these subjects and go on to win the general election. Once I won the general election, I could pursue my legislative priorities.

That was very imperfect logic to me. I let many of Mark's answers and verbiage go through at times, whether in position papers or press releases, but some I stopped as they were too over-the-top. I was left feeling less than proud of some of this, but the response from likely voters was fairly positive. Mark had appeared to gauge the voter sentiment correctly, and I found myself feeling less guilty. Maybe this was how a campaign is won.

CHAPTER 5

Getting Started

MARK RETURNED FROM HIS VACATION, I signed his contract, and we were off and running. The first orders of business were to get on the ballot—which has very specific requirements governed by the state of Ohio—and to register with the Federal Election Commission (FEC). Mark sent me guidelines about each, but it was still up to me to get both done.

The election laws in Ohio require candidates to obtain fifty signatures in order to get on the ballot. This sounds easy, but I quickly learned that there was much more to this than I thought. For starters, the fifty signers had to be "qualified electors," which meant they needed to be registered Republicans who lived in the Eighth Congressional District. In Ohio, you only become a registered Republican when you vote in a Republican Party primary. But because many people don't bother to vote in primaries, they were not eligible to sign the petition. Complicating this is that people would say they were a Republican, say they had voted in a Republican primary, and say they lived in the Eighth Congressional District, and then sign the petition. But they might not have their facts straight, which would result in their signature being invalidated. You just had no way to know for sure at the time you submit the paperwork.

This leads candidates to collect more than fifty signatures, just to be safe. However, the petition rules only allow 150 signatures to be submitted to the Board of Elections. If you submit more than 150, the board will reject the entire filing.

So here's what I did: First, I went online and found the official petition form on the Secretary of State website. I printed it double-sided on legal paper. I filled out the top with my information and signed it. Next, Mark got a list of registered Republicans in one of the district's more densely populated areas. Tricia and I then found a few close Republican friends to help with the door-to-door effort. It was already the end of November, and the filing deadline was December 16. We wanted to move quickly so we would have time to double-check all the signatures and make sure our filing would pass muster. Over the course of two weekends, we had three groups (everyone was paired up to have some company) ring doorbells and hope the registered Republican from our list was home and that he or she would sign.

Fifty signatures. That's it. What did the math really look like? On average, our groups found that when they rang doorbells, only one in three doors opened. In some houses, it was obvious no one was home (dark, quiet, no cars), but some had TVs on and didn't answer, and others barely got the curtains pulled before the group walked up on the porch. A right neighborly feeling. For every five doors that opened—one would not have the registered Republican home, one would not want to sign *any* petition, one already signed for someone else and didn't want to sign again (even though doing so is permitted), one wanted to know more and said to come back, and one agreed to sign. Every once in a while, you'd get lucky and have a double success—usually a husband and wife who were both registered and both agreed to sign. The record was four. Husband, wife, and two sons. However, the math was still about one signature for every fifteen houses where the list said a registered Republican lived. So in order to collect 150 signatures, we had to ring 2,250 doorbells.

We muddled through this for two straight weekends and then went a little overtime during the week to get there. Our final tally was 148 signatures. Tricia and I presented the petition to the Board of Elections a week ahead of time. It was a pretty big event for us. We dressed up nicely and drove together. We walked into a non-descript government building and over to the counter where a sign indicated petitions were accepted. We waited for a few minutes until a woman appeared on the other side. She looked it over said it appeared fine but would have to be checked officially, which could take a few days. We left elated and were confident that it would be fine. There were no balloons or confetti, but we already felt like I was going to win. A few days later, we got the good news. A few dozen signatures were disqualified, and a handful were illegible (even the printed name part), but overall we were well above the fifty-signature minimum.

I was in. I was officially running for U.S. Congress.

The other initial step was filing paperwork with the Federal Election Commission (FEC). The FEC is an independent agency that was created by the Federal Election Campaign Act of 1974. It was designed to make federal elections and campaigns more transparent and make sure every candidate follows the rules, particularly with regard to raising and spending money. It is overseen by six commissioners who are appointed by the president and confirmed by the Senate. The commission's 2020 budget was about $71.5 million, which seems like a lot, but they reviewed over 600 million financial transactions in the latest election, then posted these on their website. That's where most media get their information regarding campaign money raised from whom and spent on what. Given the importance of elections, it's incredible that this tiny agency is all we have as a watchdog over campaign finances.

Candidates for Congress or president must file a Statement of Candidacy with the FEC once they have raised or spent $15,000. When you file this statement, you do so under the name of your committee, which will then appear in every advertisement as part of that disclaimer at the end. You know the "Paid for by citizens for John Smith" thing you hear at the end of political advertisements? We called ours "Spurlino for Congress." Short and simple. Incidentally, this form is officially called "FEC Form 2."[7]

After you file FEC Form 2, then you file—yes, you guessed it—FEC Form 1. (I just bragged about how much the FEC does with a small budget, but now you see they are still 100 percent a federal government organization.) FEC Form 1 is the Statement of Organization.[8] On this, candidates designate their campaign treasurer and other campaign finance information. You must have a campaign treasurer before you can accept contributions or disperse funds, and the treasurer is the only person who can sign FEC reports. If needed, you can also designate an assistant treasurer. Both FEC Form 1 and Form 2 can be downloaded from the FEC website, but they must be filed in original paper form and mailed to the FEC in Washington. Subsequent reports can be filed electronically.

I was also required to file a personal financial disclosure with the clerk of the U.S. House of Representatives. This disclosure was due thirty days before the primary. This was a long form where you list assets and liabilities, but the values of most can be listed by range. That's why you might hear sometimes that a congressman has $10 million to $40 million in net worth. A normal person would think that anyone could come up with something more accurate than that, but that's the way the form is set up. The real problem is that anything without a specific value (think of the home that you bought thirty years ago or a privately owned business) isn't subject to any scrutiny, and assets in a trust or other such vehicle can be hidden. Be assured that most of our senators and representatives are worth much more than what appears on their financial disclosure forms.

Now that the "fun" regulatory stuff was taken care of, Mark and I began working on the meat of my campaign. We knew that questions would start to come from the media, and we needed to be ready. That meant I needed an official announcement of my candidacy distributed to district media and statewide reporters. This announcement would set the tone for my campaign and would emphasize my positions and differentiate me from the other candidates. It was extremely important to use specific words that voters would recognize and associate with me throughout the campaign. The announcement would also use phrases that I would repeat throughout the campaign cycle and use in advertisements and on social media.

To prepare for this, Mark and I worked on a wide range of issue briefings, my bio, the announcement event, and a script for the announcement, which would be recorded and then used, in part and whole, throughout the rest of the campaign.

Aside from this work, Mark also discussed with me the need to hire a campaign manager who would manage the day-to-day operations of the campaign. He said he had someone in mind and wanted me to meet him.

A few nights later, Mark came to my home with the proposed campaign manager—Baylor Myers. I welcomed them in, and we joined Tricia at the kitchen table. Baylor was well dressed, intelligent, and articulate. He explained that he had graduated from nearby Miami University in 2013 with a BA in history, political science, and government; was president of the Young Republicans on his campus; and now worked for Americans for Prosperity (AFP), the political organization funded by the Koch brothers. He was most recently AFP's interim state director in Ohio and wanted to do more political work, such as campaigns. He and Mark had known each other for several years, and Mark spoke highly of him.

Baylor was much younger than I had imagined a campaign manager would be. Having graduated in 2013, I figured he was twenty-five years old or so, which was young, but he looked even younger. I remember thinking he must get asked for his ID every time he buys a beer. Despite this, Baylor showed a maturity and knowledge of politics well beyond his years and looks. While somewhat reserved, he would perk up when the conversation turned to campaigning and politics, and he'd show his command of the issues. He also talked about his time working for the Mitt Romney presidential campaign here in Ohio, and I could tell he had a passion for national politics and working on campaigns.

We talked for about an hour. Everyone knew this was just an initial meeting and that Tricia and I were going to think about it. I also knew that we needed to get someone in place ASAP. Mark and Baylor left, and Tricia and I started comparing notes on what we thought. We were both impressed but also a bit surprised. His age obviously came up and the fact he lacked actual experience running a campaign. But his knowledge and passion showed through brightly. Also, Mark (and a few others I consulted with prior) had assured me this is what a campaign looks like. The campaign manager is not a grizzled old guy who has done this one hundred times. It is usually a young "kid" who can manage operations, tactics, schedule, etc. and work with the political consultant who really runs the show. (Young people will typically have more comfort with leading-edge communications technologies and platforms, though that wasn't Baylor's calling card.)

After talking some more, we both realized that we really were impressed with Baylor. We could see connecting with him, and we could see him working hard for my election. I asked Tricia if we should sleep on it, and she said, "I'm fine with him. I won't feel any different in the morning." And with that sound and trusted advice, I called Mark before he could even drop off Baylor or get home. I told him we liked Baylor and wanted to hire him. Mark shared it with Baylor, who started working as my campaign manager four days later.

CHAPTER 6

Investigating Myself

OPPOSITION RESEARCH—OR "OPPO"—IS a staple of most political campaigns. It's carried out to see if there is anything to exploit about a candidate's rivals that would make him or her less appealing to their voter base; the intention for this information is to bring it up at strategic times in the race—usually during debates or forums or in interviews or shared with the media.

But my introduction to oppo came shortly after hiring Mark. He asked if we could spend $1,000 to research *me*. He said that there was a good chance someone would do this on me anyway, and it was a good idea to get ahead of anything bad or sensitive. Then, he asked me the obvious question: "Is there anything you want to talk about now or that you expect we will find?"

I hadn't given anything like this a thought and was still processing the other campaigns. We were poring over all the competition for some tidbits of embarrassment or better (worse?) yet, a smoking gun or skeleton in the closet. I hesitated and tried to think what there might be. Of course, we've all done things we regret and that would be embarrassing to see in print, but most of that seemed to be from teenage years or college. I'm not a saint, but nothing really stood out in my mind.

I made a few guesses and told him about being married twice before, a partner who sued me, and some union stuff from my company, but that was really it. I told him to go ahead and run the search and see what comes up.

There are a few typical ways to do oppo research. Usually, it involves a deep dive into whatever public information is available through Google, LexisNexis, and any number of background check firms. There are apparently several other avenues that are more "deep web" stuff, but I think Mark stuck to the basics given the price tag.

A few days later, he called with the report and gave me the highlights. Afterward, he emailed over the report. It was a whole page and a half.

Here is what he found:

- Two minor traffic citations, and a few speeding tickets.
- A state tax lien release from Wyoming. This was a lien on me personally for $753 in taxes that my company was late paying. I never understood how Wyoming got away with a lien on me personally for that, but it was paid long ago.
- I had voted in five of the six previous general elections and hadn't voted in a primary for five years.
- A lawsuit for gender bias in the sale of a vehicle when I owned a car dealership. I was named personally even though I never had any knowledge about the matter. There were some remarks attributed to me that were not very complimentary,

but I never said them. It was typical of lawsuits that the plaintiffs can state anything they want, whether true or not, and there are no ramifications for it. The case was settled.

- A lawsuit from a former business partner showing it was closed. The case was settled.
- Two divorces.
- The divorce docket from my first wife had a notation about psychological testing scores. It sounds ominous, but when children are involved (my two daughters) and they evaluate custody, all courts do psychological tests.
- Two donations to Democrats. One for $500 to Senator Sherrod Brown (hoping for access, which I got with a staffer) and one for $100 to David Pepper when he ran for state auditor. His father, John Pepper, is a friend.

None of this seemed very exciting to me, and I assumed Mark was happy, but he questioned me about the gender bias lawsuit. I couldn't recall any of the details but remembered my dealership treating a woman unfairly, and when I got all the details from the general manager who ran the dealership, we immediately made it right with her and settled. I also remember chastising my general manager about it and let him know it was to never happen again.

Mark appeared satisfied with all this but wanted to go over the gender bias lawsuit again to make sure he knew what I would say about it if questioned. I assured him I wasn't at the dealership regularly and wasn't running it. In any case, we settled on the truth. I was unaware of the bias and made it right as soon as I knew about it.

The other thing he wanted to cover was the donations to Democrats. I pointed out that it was only $600 and that the $500 donation to Senator Brown was connected to my wanting to talk to him about some legislation focused on helping infants.

Mark also dug up some material from the National Labor Relations Board (NLRB). I had several run-ins with them regarding our Teamster workforce in Indianapolis and apparently had a bit of a reputation. Mark found an NLRB publication that called me a "bad actor." This refers to an individual or company that has been accused of acting in bad faith, violating labor laws, or not complying with NLRB rulings. None of it was true, and I told Mark we should exploit it if it was brought up. He seemed to think I should be a little less cavalier about these matters. I agreed but thought I would probably never be able to come off as anything but proud of my company's actions in light of how the Teamsters and NLRB had acted at the time.

Throughout the campaign, nothing related to what I've just detailed ever came up. Only once did someone post something on my Facebook page regarding my time as a car dealer that might have been in reference to the lawsuit, but Baylor simply removed the post and blocked the person. It was a nonevent.

We also never ran oppo on anyone else. Mark had asked about it, but I felt strongly that it was not money well spent, and I didn't want to run negative against others. I truly believed that it made the most sense to run positive on me, on my message, and why I should be elected. I had no interest in the negative game, although Mark assured me that it would be necessary once we gained traction and identified my most formidable competition.

CHAPTER 7

Announcing and Filming

A FEW WEEKS AFTER I hired Mark, he took some time to explain more about the announcement. Candidates issued formal announcements for their campaigns in various ways—some simply shared press releases, some did nothing, and others, like myself, capitalized on the moment for media exposure and building out a campaign narrative by filming and scripting an event. Mark said he would write up a script, we would film for an entire day, and then we would edit it together. Aside from the video, we would be creating still shots to be used for the rest of the campaign. The video itself would appear on my campaign's website and YouTube the day I officially announced. It would all be professionally filmed, with Mark as director.

Mark and I talked on and off for a few days while he was working on the script. He had a clear idea in mind of how he wanted it to come off. I would be the outsider and preach about career politicians in Washington, DC. It would also hit the tried-and-true Republican primary issues where he had been pulling me to the right.

After some back and forth—and cajoling on his part—here is where we landed:

> *I'm Jim Spurlino. I'm not a professional politician. In fact, I've never run for office before.*
>
> *I'm a husband, father, and small business owner, and I'm worried about what the professional politicians are doing to our country. Their **greed** and **political games** are hurting the hard-working people at my company, and they are hurting families like yours and mine.*
>
> *Over the years, I've tried to encourage politicians to do the right thing for our country and for families who are just trying to help their kids and grandkids have a better life than they had.*
>
> *I've watched other people take office, and I've hoped that they would put the **national** interest ahead of the special interests. But they **don't**. I've **tried** to work with professional politicians. Although I'm a conservative Republican, I've even encouraged **Democrats** to vote for the right policies.*
>
> *But many politicians expect a campaign contribution before they'll even meet with you. Congress has become a place where people like you and I have to pay an admission fee just to get inside. I know—I've tried. But **nothing** gets done.*
>
> *Within hours of John Boehner's announcement that he was resigning from Congress, professional politicians began lining up to advance their career and replace him. I watched and waited to see if someone from the world of business and common sense would come forward. But no one did.*
>
> *That's why I've decided to step aside from my family business and run for Congress. The professional politicians drew the lines of the eighth district to benefit **themselves**. It's a southwest and*

western Ohio district, but the boundary lines snake every which way to meet the political needs of the ruling class.

Luckily, the Founding Fathers anticipated that professional politicians would try and use district lines to keep some people from running for office. That's why the Constitution says that **anyone** *from our community can run for this seat—whether or not they live within the special lines drawn by the incumbent officeholders.*

I've lived in this area all my life. I employ more than one hundred people through my business in Butler County, the biggest part of this district. Our company helps build homes, businesses, and even churches all across this district. **No one** *knows this area better than I do.*

When I was young, my father taught me how to build strong foundations. I started at the bottom, and I learned every job from the bottom up firsthand. I wore out countless pairs of workmen's pants and shoes doing that difficult work. I worked my way up through a company for fifteen years and then started my own company. And I've helped many other companies get off the ground and employ people—right here in Ohio.

When I look at the people who are in Congress, I see a lot of lawyers, former government staffers, and countless professional politicians. I don't see many people who've worked at construction sites, as I have.

I don't see many people who've built a business and met a payroll, as **I** *do every week.*

And, in Congress, I don't see many people who are looking out for the everyday man and woman who just want to make a living and provide for their family.

In a way, the brilliant men who wrote our Declaration of Independence and Constitution were—like me—in the concrete business. They laid the foundation for a great nation. It was hard work. But they knew that future generations would build the walls and rooms of our American structure, so they took the time to make sure the foundation was solid.

*The professional politician class is chipping away at our national foundation. They move to Washington and **become** Washington. They forget that our government was designed to be a **limited** government. And—worst of all—most of them wake up every morning with **one** thing in mind: how they can advance their own careers.*

*This year, one congressman from Michigan announced his re-election bid for the twenty-seventh time. That's right—he's been in Congress since in 1965. He's been in Washington longer than some of the **monuments**!*

*If you elect me to represent you in Congress, here's one thing you'll know for sure: I might **work** in Washington, but I won't **become** Washington. My home, my family, and my business will stay right here in our community. Luckily, I have other people who can run this company and continue the good work we do.*

I feel called to help lead this nation in the United States House of Representatives. If you want to know more about me before you vote, here are just a few things for you to consider:

- *I'm a conservative Republican. I think Ronald Reagan was one of our greatest presidents. Today's leaders can learn a lot from President Reagan's guidance.*
- *I'm **pro-life**. I believe life begins at conception, and I believe Planned Parenthood shouldn't get a **nickel** of taxpayer money.*

- *I'm a proud gun owner and strong supporter of gun rights. Here's my concealed carry permit.*
- *I'll fight to unwind the mess caused by Obamacare. We can improve our health-care system with **patient-centered** and market-based solutions, not Washington bureaucrats meddling in your private medical issues.*
- *I support traditional marriage between one man and one woman.*
- *I think we're taxed too much. Every tax intrudes more government power into your life. We need to **tax** less and **spend** less. I'll support a simplified tax that will put the IRS out of business and make the tax burden fairer for everyone.*

*If someone with these conservative views is what **you** want in your next member of Congress, I hope you'll join me.*

If someone who's avoided the gamesmanship and bickering of professional politics is the kind of congressman you think our nation needs, I hope you'll join me.

And, if you're starting to worry that after seven years of Barack Obama you don't recognize your country anymore, that it needs conservative leaders who think that America is the greatest nation on Earth, I hope you'll join me.

Go to my website, VoteSpurlino to sign up and help us win the March 15 election.

I'm Jim Spurlino. I'm not a professional politician. I'm a conservative Republican. And I ask for your support.

Thank you.

I wasn't thrilled about the pro-life and traditional marriage parts, but Mark is a good cajoler and did convince me that it aligned with my personal beliefs and would help get me elected. I thought the script was the tough part, but once this was finalized there was a lot of work left to do.

We started out with selecting the location of the video shoot. It needed to reflect the district and conservative values. Mark had in mind a local business in a manufacturing setting. He also told me that he would like to have thirty to fifty supporters there to be the "crowd." I thought the petition was hard, but this sounded worse. After some thought, I contacted a friend who was in senior management at a very large contracting firm and was also a customer of mine. They had a large shop nearby at their headquarters that would be perfect. It had a maintenance area that was as big as a football field, with overhead cranes, forklifts, welders, and all other kinds of manufacturing stuff you'd find in the heartland of Ohio. In addition, they had just held a large company-wide meeting, which involved building a stage from which the company's leaders spoke. They hadn't dismantled it yet and said we could use it. That was almost too easy.

From there, we moved on to arranging for the shooting of the "B-roll," which refers to scenes created and filmed so they could be used for other purposes. I was a little surprised at how elaborate this was to be. These B-roll scenes would include:

- A scene of me talking to and reading a book to small children to show my interest in early childhood and education issues
- A scene of me talking to a doctor in a doctor's office to show my interest in health care, particularly at a time when Obamacare was a hot-button issue

- A scene of me talking to a senior citizen with prescription bottles on a table to show my interest in seniors as well as the cost of prescription drugs
- A scene of me in a business meeting to reinforce my status as a business owner and decision-maker
- A scene of me on a construction site to show my background in construction material and economic development
- A scene of me and a friend hunting with shotguns to underscore my commitment to the Second Amendment and my comfort with guns

The day came to film, and Mark showed up at my house early in the morning. He wanted to go through my closet and pick out clothes for each scene. It was a little odd having another man in my closet telling what clothes I was going to wear. I just went with it.

Mark followed Tricia and I over to where we were to film. All the scenes would take place somewhere on that property. We started with the announcement video. Tricia and my friend had help finding the "crowd," and everyone was assembled, drinking coffee, and eating donuts. I felt like a celebrity as I walked in. I knew most of them but not all. I found it amazing that someone who had never met me would give up their Saturday morning to come to this filming. Everyone seemed excited, and their energy was contagious as I shook hands and chatted with them. Then, it was off to makeup!

While some nice woman was trying to make me look good in the makeup chair, Mark asked me if I had ever used a teleprompter. I looked at him like he was crazy. He said we were going to use one today and it was no big deal and I should just read from it naturally. He also reminded to look back and forth and use both teleprompter screens so it looked natural. None of this seemed natural, but I nodded.

Once out on the stage, I was nervous and pumped up at once. The crowd was into it. Mark helped them practice cheering and clapping and told them they could do either one spontaneously throughout the speech. He told them about me and why I was running. He was effectively my opening act, warming up the crowd, and it seemed to be going well.

All in all, we probably did about ten takes, some from the beginning and most from different parts. Mark was after just the right tone and emphasis in different areas. I also was struggling a bit with the teleprompter and looking natural. In the end, we got enough good takes to wrap that up. I was most impressed with the crowd. They were clapping and reacting, even making a few encouraging comments here and there. I ended up enjoying it quite a bit.

It was now on to the other scenes. There would not be any audio, so it was mostly just play acting and mouthing things like "peas and carrots" to make it look like a conversation. Tricia had lined up friends with about ten kids aged three to six years old for the first shoot. I sat on a little chair in a conference room and read to them. The kids were kids and fun to have there. Their parents all seemed to be very proud of having them in the video except for one family friend Tricia had invited. This young mother had grown up with our older children and had always been very close to us. Now, as a young professional with two young children herself, she had developed her own political philosophy, and it was decidedly liberal. Apparently, my thoughts on the political issues of the day did not match up so well with her own, and she decided that her young daughters were not going to be in the video. It was the first of several times in my campaign where someone surprised us with a strong negative reaction.

Next was Tricia's older friend, Phyllis. She was playing a doctor and had a lab coat on. She was great, and we dubbed her "Dr. Phyl" as she took to the role with aplomb. We stood and talked near the reception counter. Then we moved on to the break room and talking to my friend's elderly father with about six prescription bottles in front of us. We were to appear to be talking about the high price of prescription drugs and Medicare. All the time, Mark was telling us to look this way, smile, pick this up and comment, and of course, "act natural!"

We broke for lunch and then moved into a conference room, at which point I changed into a suit for my fifth clothing change of the day. I looked like I was running a meeting and pointing to some report. The remaining scenes were filmed outside. The first shoot was me helping a crew pour concrete and then talking to the workers. I had my hard hat and Carhartt jacket on. Next, we filmed the hunting scene. My friend and I had on camouflage (which Tricia had bought me the day before), and I had a borrowed shotgun. We staged it along some overgrown shrubs and walked like we were out hunting and talking. Lastly, we went to a large field with an earth embankment on one side. I had my Glock 19, a 9mm gun with ten rounds in the magazine. Mark also wanted me to have another magazine in my pocket. The idea was to film me shooting ten bullets quickly, drop the magazine out of the gun, pop the next magazine in, and resume shooting. We only did this shot twice. I think the neighbors probably didn't appreciate the noise, and it felt a little like a Terminator movie.

As an aside, the reaction I got from all these videos was almost all positive. I guess it mostly showed me doing the things I have done in my life and looked real enough. It was tiring but a blast to shoot. Mark spent the next week or so editing, and the final version and B-roll footage was excellent and very professional looking. I looked forward to getting it out to the public as quickly as possible.

CHAPTER 8

The Budget

WITH THE BIG VIDEO SHOOT day complete, I was looking forward to talking to voters and businesses about how to make our nation stronger and more prosperous. I liked doing this in town halls and other settings where people wanted to hear from the candidates. I liked having discussions with voters, hearing their concerns, and then offering my thoughts and solutions. A lot of commonsense stuff to me. It felt totally in my wheelhouse.

But before I could get to this, Mark and I had another conversation about what my campaign would look like going forward. Of course, before he could get started, I wanted to know more about the budget. Mark had previously given me a budget of what he called primary expenditures. It looked like this:

Primary Budget ESTIMATE	December	January	February	March
Announcement Video/ Filming	$24,000	$ -	$ -	$ -
Website	$10,000	$ -	$ -	$ -
VOIP	$ -	$8,500	$3,000	$3,000
Consultant	$10,000	$10,000	$10,000	$10,000
AB Chase	$ -	$ -	$3,000	$3,000
Telephone Townhall	$ -	$ -	$ -	$5,000
Signs	$ -	$ -	$3,000	$ -
Political Director	$ -	$4,500	$4,500	$4,500
Manager	$7,500	$7,500	$7,500	$7,500
FEC Compliance Firm	$2,000	$2,000	$2,000	$2,000
Handout Piece	$ -	$7,000	$ -	$ -
Low-level Digital Ads	$5,000	$2,500	$2,500	$2,500
Poll	$ -	$25,000	$ -	$ -
TOTALS	**$58,500**	**$67,000**	**$35,500**	**$37,500**
GRAND TOTAL				**$198,500**

It definitely looked manageable to me, and I felt there would be no problem raising this amount of money. Having spent time with industry association Political Action Committees (PACs) and giving some money to candidates in the past, this seemed very doable. However, now Mark wanted to share what he thought was a more realistic budget for what it would take to win. He said he had given it more thought and considered the other candidates and possible support they could generate. "None of this was sure or a given," he said, "but if you want to make sure you are competitive and have a real chance to win this thing, then this is what a budget looks like." And with that, he sent me a new budget, and it wasn't anything like the first one.

Primary Budget REVISED	December	January	February	March	Comments
Manager	$7,500	$7,500	$7,500	$7,500	
Consultant	$10,000	$10,000	$10,000	$10,000	
Polling	$15,000	$10,000	$5,000	$5,000	Short benchmark, brushfire, tracking
Announcement Video	$10,000	$ -	$ -	$ -	May reduce overall TV production
Webpage	$10,000	$ -	$ -	$ -	
Field/VOIP Program	$10,000	$15,000	$20,000	$15,000	Could go down if few volunteers
Direct Mail	$141,000	$131,600	$37,600	$84,600	R4s, senior citizens, gun owners, pro-life
AB Chase Program	$ -	$ -	$5,000	$5,000	Pair with VOIP calls
Pandora Radio	$30,000	$40,000	$50,000	$75,000	
Cable TV	$75,000	$125,000	$300,000	$200,000	
Broadcast TV Dayton	$ -	$50,000	$100,000	$200,000	2,000 spots
Broadcast TV Cincinnati	$ -	$75,000	$125,000	$250,000	2,000 spots
Radio	$50,000	$15,000	$200,000	$15,000	
TV Production	$30,000	$40,000	$40,000	$ -	
Radio Production	$15,000	$20,000	$20,000	$ -	
Teletown Halls	$ -	$ -	$5,000	$5,000	One to AB Chase and one 3/14
Google Ads	$ -	$ -	$10,000	$20,000	Large focus on GOTV
Facebook Ads	$10,000	$20,000	$30,000	$30,000	Sidebar ads and promoted posts
Signs	$ -	$ -	$3,000	$ -	20" x 30"
Pre-roll Ads	$10,000	$20,000	$30,000	$50,000	
TOTALS	**$423,500**	**$579,100**	**$998,100**	**$972,100**	
GRAND TOTAL				**$2,972,800**	

I was expecting a modest increase in the second budget—not one that was *fifteen times* larger.

I told Mark I'd call him back after I reviewed it, but the truth was that I had looked at it enough to be pissed. How did we get started down this path with verbal conversations that included $500,000 to $750,000, then we had a basic budget of $200,000, and then we ended up with one that was nearly $3 million?! I tried not to think he intentionally misled me. But it was hard for me to fathom what had changed to justify such an exponential change in the budget. (Mark never offered an explanation I could accept for this shift.) Best case, he miscommunicated or had some new thinking about the race that wasn't relevant previously. Either way, I was unhappy.

A few days later, we talked again, and I expressed my shock. Mark backpedaled a bit, saying we could cut some things and maybe get down to $2 million, which was still *ten times* the original budget. He also said we'd spend what we raised and make the best of it (*Obviously*, I thought). He probed me a bit on where I might be able to raise money. He asked about my family and particularly my dad. I could tell he had done some online research and knew my dad was fairly wealthy. "Would he give you $1 million? To see his son in Congress?"

"No," I answered confidently, "there is no way. I doubt he'd give a dime." He then asked a few personal questions that I didn't feel like getting into, but I told him my dad rarely—if ever—gave to political campaigns, and he was a liberal anyway.

Mark pivoted to friends. He asked, "How about friends? You've lived here all your life. There must be some wealthy friends, or friends of friends, you could tap?" I thought about it and there were certainly some, but I couldn't foresee them providing significant amounts. Then, we went on to my industry. He said, "You're well known in your industry. Are there executives or companies that would support you? Could you raise $1 million there?" I felt there was a chance to raise a lot of money that way, but I doubted that it would approach $1 million.

I was being conservative in my estimates on what I could raise but also wanted to make sure to underpromise. Frankly, I just wasn't sure. After relating my pessimism, we went on to discuss two alternatives. One was the possibility of hiring an individual to fundraise, and the other was whether an industry Super PAC might be a good strategy to tap into corporate funds.

We explored the fundraising person for a brief time. Baylor knew someone who had worked for Speaker of the House Paul Ryan. This seemed impressive, and we set up a time for me to talk with her. I had a conversation with her, and we didn't hit it off, but I felt I needed help and the Ryan connection was a big deal. Mark eventually proposed several options to her that ranged from straight salary to more commission-based. She eventually turned it down altogether. We did not explore hiring anyone else for two primary reasons. First, I learned that anyone filling this role was essentially going to organize lists of possible donors and then make sure that I made calls to solicit money. That was really it: we were paying someone to nag me to make phone calls. Second, I was not so impressed with the credentials of the person we interviewed. She didn't have campaign fundraising experience, she didn't ask about my fundraising plan, and she had an all-knowing attitude (despite knowing very little). While she worked for Ryan for several years, upon closer questioning, it appeared that she was primarily a nanny to Ryan's children. I was certain I didn't need a nag or a nanny, even if they were the same person.

To explore the idea of a Super PAC, I needed to understand them fully myself. According to the FEC, "Super PACs are independent expenditure-only political committees that may receive unlimited contributions from individuals, corporations, labor unions, and other political action committees for the purpose of financing independent expenditures and other independent political activity. The committee will not use those funds to make contributions, whether direct, in-kind, or via coordinated communications, to federal candidates or committees."[9] In other words, a Super PAC can raise any amount of money from anyone or anything. There are no maximums, and it can receive money from companies. They also don't have to disclose the source of their funding. The big caveat is that they cannot talk to campaigns or candidates about how they spend their money.

Mark put it this way: find an industry executive willing to spearhead this, and he would assign one of his employees to manage it. Mark and the employee would just have to put up a "firewall." Even though this guy worked for Mark and had an office next to his, they would never talk about my campaign. Mark said that's how "everyone" does it. It certainly didn't feel right, and I got a better understanding of why most people are suspicious of Super PACs!

I made a few calls to CEOs I knew in my industry and found some interest. One CEO thought it was a great idea and offered to help lead this effort. In the end, he emailed 371 fellow executives across the country and asked them to support the new Super PAC, which was called "Americans for Concrete Solutions." Very catchy for a candidate from the concrete industry! Along with our industry's national association, this new Super PAC planned a fundraising event. Coincidentally, our industry's annual convention was being held in Las Vegas the following month. The plan was to sponsor a reception during the convention and invite all the CEOs in attendance. It was perfect timing and an invite went out a few weeks before the event.

Tricia and I flew to Vegas, and I spent some time walking the convention center and socializing with everyone. It was a well-attended convention, with about 80,000 attendees. I was among my peers, many whom I had known for years. By then, it was common knowledge that I was running, and most whom I talked to were thrilled to have "one of our own" possibly going to Congress. Even companies who did not do business with me, for whom I did business with their competitors, were supportive.

As I walked, I would get greeted every few minutes. A short conversation, pats on the back, and more than a few promises to send a check. Nowhere else during the campaign would I feel the sense of "home" and belonging that I felt there. It was good to be with "my people."

After six or so hours of walking, we went to Piero's Italian Cuisine for the reception. It was just a few blocks from the convention center, and about fifty CEOs or presidents of major and large companies were present.

During the reception, I made my usual remarks and explained why I would make a great congressman. Of course, it was a room full of friends and friendly acquaintances, so I anticipated it would go over well. The plan was for me to talk for about fifteen minutes and then leave the building. That way, the Super PAC could then make a plea for big dollars from this group and not be coordinating with me or my campaign. All perfectly legal, but it still didn't feel that way.

While we had high hopes of possibly raising $500,000 to $1 million, the Super PAC only ended up raising $111,000. (I found this out after the election by checking their FEC-required disclosures.) We also raised about $45,000 from reception attendees who donated to my campaign as individuals. Of the $45,000, there were six donations of $2,700 each, which is the legal limit set by the FEC. All in all, it was a pretty good night. I seriously doubt any other candidate in this race raised $160,000 total in one night, so I was quite pleased.

Besides my one great fundraising night, there were also two events organized in my congressional district that were similar but without the benefit of a national convention to boost attendance and recognition. In each case, a good friend and business associate helped organize and invite people. One was held in the conference room of a local hotel, and the other was in a local business office. While only about twenty people showed up to each, both were still a positive show of support, and we ended up raising about $50,000.

There is one donation that stands out from all others though. After one evening of meeting potential voters, an older gentleman followed Tricia and me out to the parking lot. His name was John and we had seen him at a few other events. I'm guessing he was in his mid to late seventies and liked to talk politics. He also was turning into quite a supporter, always taking time to introduce me to a few others he knew. This one evening, he asked if Tricia and I would like to meet his "coffee club," which was a group of friends who met at 6:30 a.m. each morning at their local McDonald's. He said it would be a great opportunity to meet others. I agreed to the meeting, and then John asked if I could show up the following morning. I agreed to that as well, even though I wouldn't be getting home until about 11:00 p.m. and this McDonald's was about an hour away from our house.

When Tricia and I arrived the following morning at 6:30 a.m., John walked out to the parking lot to greet us. He seemed very happy to see us. We walked in and there were about ten other senior citizens sipping coffee and nibbling on some food over in a corner. John introduced everyone, and I sat down and started chatting with one table. Over the course of about an hour and a half, I moved through the table and talked to everyone, as did Tricia. It was good conversation, even if it wasn't the best use of my time. I hoped for some votes but doubted there was a contribution to get here.

As Tricia and I got up to leave, thanking everyone as we did, one of the other gentlemen got up and walked out with us. When out in the parking lot as Tricia continued to the car, he gently put one hand on my arm to stop me and said, "I really liked everything you said. We need more people like you running for office, and we need you to win. My wife and I are both retired and living on Social Security and a little pension. We don't have much but I want you to have this." And with that, he reached over with his palm down and handed me a twenty-dollar bill. Just like one might try and bribe a maître d' for a table. He smiled, wished me luck, and turned to go back in McDonald's. I was moved beyond words.

CHAPTER 9

The Frontrunner Steps Aside

THE FIRST MAJOR SHOCK OF the campaign did not take long to happen. On Friday, December 18—two days after the filing deadline to enter the race—Roger Reynolds dropped out of the race. Reynolds was the Butler County auditor and a local favorite in the most populous county in the district. He was a CPA and had spent the last seven years in that job. He had declared his candidacy within a few weeks of Boehner making his big announcement, but he was out just over two months later.

Reynolds had raised $200,000 in that very short time and had almost won the Butler County GOP endorsement in what would have been a major leg up on his opponents. Reynolds also had received an early endorsement from Congressman Mike Turner in neighboring Dayton and was receiving unofficial help from Boehner in the form of staff and advice.

Reynolds was assembling a strong team to help his campaign. He was meeting with Rex Elsass, a highly influential and successful political strategist who had honed his skills for twenty years in Ohio and throughout the country. His early career success had made him the unofficial leader of the "nasty boys"—a young group of political operatives known for heckling opponents at events and once leaving a dead chicken on a candidate's doorstep (he later denied knowing about the chicken).

But the budding relationship between Reynolds and Elsass came to end that fall. Elsass was insisting that Reynolds use media controlled by Elsass, and Reynolds resisted. Reynolds eventually blew up, and the relationship was off. Elsass was so well known and respected that this news spread fast and resulted in another candidate, Tim Derickson, seeking out Elsass's assistance within hours of hearing the news and then hiring him.

How "good" was Elsass? Shortly after being enlisted by Derickson, who was widely recognized as the nicest guy running, Elsass's team dug into opposition research on Reynolds.

On December 17, Reynolds was attending the Butler County GOP Christmas party. He was in his home county among friends, enjoying his status as frontrunner and looking for more support and money from the crowd. He even tweeted a photo of himself at the party. But, during the party, Reynolds was apparently handed an envelope, and it wasn't from an invited guest.

The very next day, he released a statement saying he was withdrawing from the race. "The balance of family responsibilities and commitment to the job is delicate for all parents, including elected officials. When I made the decision to run twelve weeks ago, I was confident I could balance the family needs of raising two teenage daughters with the needs of the campaign and ultimately the responsibilities as congressman. I now realize a healthy balance is not possible, and my family must take priority," his statement read.

At the time, there was a lot of speculation about the reason for Reynolds's abrupt overnight reversal of course—from full-on campaigning one evening, to announcing the next day that obligations to family were irreconcilable with staying in the race. Some believed it had something to do with Elsass and his opposition research.

When announcing his withdrawal from the race, Reynolds endorsed Derickson, clearing the way for the other Butler County career politician to make his run, and he seemingly put the whole race on different footing. It would make it a wide open primary, indeed.

The difficult thing to balance was how Derickson, an extremely polite state representative from a rural part of the district, would have countenanced such use of opposition research. One possibility is that Elsass and his team were freelancing this move, but this is speculation unlikely to ever be confirmed.

Interestingly, I was originally referred to Elsass and was told he was the best political consultant but also a "win at all costs" type. I didn't know for sure what that meant but could obviously guess. I was looking forward to meeting him, but he had already signed up with Reynolds at the time. I have wondered what could have been had I hired him—but I'm glad I didn't have to find out.

CHAPTER 10

Searching for Staff and Cash

I HAD A LOT OF great friends in my industry, particularly among the members of the National Ready Mix Concrete Association (NRMCA). Thanks to the NRMCA, I had gotten to know CEOs and other C-suite executives from all over the country. Many of them were quite supportive from the beginning of my campaign. I think they viewed me as a chance to see "one of theirs" in Congress. As I reached out to many of them, they donated money to my campaign, while also giving advice and making introductions that I did not expect. One of these started out from an email exchange.

Kerri Leininger was the vice president of government affairs for the NRMCA. Her role, like others with the same title, was to develop relationships with members of Congress and advocate for issues important to our industry and to business in general. Kerri has great energy and a lot of experience in political circles, including having worked for Senator Mitch McConnell. She started by reaching out to her McConnell contacts to inquire about Boehner's intentions after Roger Reynolds dropped out of the race.

After confirming that Boehner had sent a team of staffers to work for the Reynolds campaign, she worked to find out what would happen to that team in the wake of his announcement and whether Boehner would support or even endorse someone else. After some emails and calls to friends, she told me that Boehner was going to stay out of the campaign. That led Baylor to see if he could recruit anyone from the Reynolds campaign. First on the list was the former Reynolds volunteer chair, who had organized and directed all the volunteers in his campaign. Baylor met with him twice. He was nice enough but seemed depleted of energy and reluctant to get involved with another campaign. It was a shame, as we thought he could have brought several volunteers with him.

Next, Baylor found a former Boehner campaign manager who had become a political advisor to Reynolds. We both met with him at Bob Evans for breakfast. He was generous with his time and thoughts but never revealed much of substance. He too had had enough politics for now and was not looking to get involved in another campaign, at least not this one. Baylor and I took mental notes of his suggestions and thanked him for his time. This was another good meeting, but nothing much was gained.

Baylor and I both continued to contact friends and acquaintances to see what we could turn up. For me, this spurred a series of emails about other possible contacts on the national side of politics. The first two suggestions came from another friend of mine in the industry.

He suggested we reach out to Tom Donohue with the U.S. Chamber of Commerce. We made a few attempts to reach out to him, but there was either no interest in the race or no interest in supporting my candidacy. I did learn later that other candidates had meetings with the chamber, but it appears they never had an interest in getting involved with a specific candidate.

I had higher hopes with the second suggestion: John Sununu. He is the former governor of New Hampshire and former White House chief of staff under George H. W. Bush. He was also a friend of our industry—NRMCA had employed him as a consultant for several years in our research work being done at the Massachusetts Institute of Technology (MIT). I had met Sununu a few times but doubted he'd remember me. A fellow industry CEO let Sununu know of my candidacy, and we hoped it would lead to something, either more connections or money. It may have helped, but we never did hear of any direct assistance one way or the other.

Eventually, Kerri provided another contact name. In her time working for McConnell, she mentioned that her first boss, Steven Law, was one of the founders of American Crossroads. I was floored and wondered how this hadn't come up earlier.

American Crossroads is a Super PAC that was founded by Law, Karl Rove, and Ed Gillespie. Rove is a political consultant who worked for George W. Bush during his elections and was also his senior advisor and deputy chief of staff in the White House. He is considered the architect of Bush's political wins and had significant influence over the work at American Crossroads. Gillespie is also a political consultant who worked for Bush and was counselor to the president during his time in office.

American Crossroads was known to have significant influence in the several elections since its 2010 founding. It often spent hundreds of millions of dollars in an election cycle, and if a campaign won its support, the result could be more contributions from other

Super PACs or just regular voters. Backing from them could mean a significant (and even election-changing) difference. My excitement was short lived, as Law told Kerri that they were not getting involved in this race at the primary level. Law then referred us to a consultant who was handling races for the U.S. House leadership. This was another positive connection, but the consultant told us he was not getting involved in the primary either.

Many other organizations and influencers were not interested in becoming involved in primaries. I could understand this as a general policy, but in this particular primary race it did not make sense to me, since the winner of the primary was a lock to be the next congressman. It seemed like the perfect primary in which to get involved, since doing so would mean determining who would be the congressman.

Kerri consoled me that my name was getting out to "the top people in town" and that, at the very minimum, they were hearing about me. I made my case about the missed opportunity, but it was to no avail. I believe, in the end, that my name was mentioned but no action was seriously considered.

After these near misses, Baylor made a renewed effort to draw on his contacts. Before joining my campaign, he was Ohio deputy director for Americans for Prosperity (AFP). AFP is an advocacy organization that was funded by the billionaire Koch brothers, David and Charles (David has since died). AFP was known to have spent as much as $37 million in an election cycle on conservative ideas and is largely credited with making the Tea Party a nationally recognized movement. While AFP did not spend direct money on candidates, an entity known as Aegis Strategic apparently had access to Koch money as well as other wealthy, like-minded individuals.

Baylor made some calls and found the person at Aegis who identified the candidates whom the group might support. He set up a lunch at a Marriott near the Cincinnati airport.

Joe Burgan looked everything like a political operative. He was impeccably dressed and well spoken. We sat down at a white-tableclothed table in the Marriott's main dining room overlooking the Ohio River. It felt like a very important meeting. We exchanged greetings and Baylor and Burgan caught up on their shared connections. Then we started talking about the primary and my candidacy. Baylor had briefed him on me and my positions, so it was more confirmation than anything. I think he was making sure I was a real person who could "walk the talk" and look the part. Overall, the meeting went very well, and as it was winding up, Burgan said he liked everything he read about me and enjoyed the conversation. He added that I was the type of candidate Aegis looks for.

As we got up and Burgan was about to head back to the airport, he said, "We like to make decisions quickly. We're a small shop, and it doesn't take long to decide. I'll be back to you in a few days." We walked to the entrance together and then went our separate ways, with Baylor and I headed to my car. Once we got in, there was a look between us as if we just stumbled onto a bag of money. I said, "Well, that seemed to go well." He replied, "Oh, hell yes that went well!"

The rest of the week allowed me to focus a bit less on the pressures of fundraising and devote my energies to setting up meetings with voters. I slacked off a bit making calls and bugging people for donations. *Help was on the way*, I thought to myself. Alas, like every other lifeline I thought was being thrown my way, we got the same old news, although this time it was with a twist.

No, Aegis would not be funding me. They said they liked me, and I was the type of candidate they looked for, but Burgan told Baylor that their friends at the Club for Growth, another similar political organization, were already supporting another candidate in this primary, and they did not want to compete with them. The reality of his explanation was that Aegis and Club for Growth often look for the same attributes in candidates to support. When one steps into a race first, they are very unlikely to fund a competitor. They feel their resources are better spent elsewhere.

I was getting pretty good at accepting bad news regarding influential people and big donations. I knew I was going to have to step up my own efforts to raise money. I also knew that I would need to revisit the conversation I had had with Mark about putting my own money into the campaign. That was not something I wanted to do, but at that point I knew I was probably going to have to.

CHAPTER 11

The Campaigning Begins

MY CAMPAIGN TEAM HAD COME together, and I was excited to start meeting with voters, talk about issues, get my new video out, and tell people how I could make a difference. It was late December, about a month since I made my decision, and the delay between that and engaging with people seemed like it took forever. The delay was caused by something I never thought about, or more precisely, what voters don't think about: politics around the holidays. Mark warned me that there would be a lull. "Nothing much happens between now and New Year's," he said. He recommended that I focus on making contact with people I knew and raising money where I could. "January is when the real work begins," he told me.

Well, this kind of sucks, I thought. After all the time spent thinking about running, making the decision, and then putting the team and video together, it was a letdown. I felt like I had been training for the Olympics, and now it was delayed a month. I kept my spirits up as best I could, but it was disheartening. Tricia and I spent time at holiday parties and trying to be active socially. Any chance to see people and tell them I was running was a plus.

January rolled around, and my calendar started filling up. Baylor began by making appointments for me to meet with the chairman of every county's Republican Party. That meant six different meetings with people I had never met but who were likely to be influential in the election. Neither Mark nor Baylor felt these meetings would amount to anything significant, but they nonetheless saw them as something that needed to be done—a "kiss the ring" type thing. I was showing respect, and the introductory meeting was also a way of showing that I was serious. The career politicians I was running against already knew most—if not all—of the chairmen, and the other novices were not likely to know this was something expected of candidates.

The most populous county took on the greatest emphasis, so Butler County was first. Baylor set up the meeting and explained that the chairman was the grandson of another former chair of the same county. This individual, whom I had met several times, ran the county's Republican Party with quite a bit of flair and always found ways to keep himself in the spotlight. The meeting with his grandson, a homebuilder and the current chairman, was set up at a bagel shop late one morning. Baylor and I arrived fifteen minutes early and went in and grabbed some coffee and a table. About thirty minutes later, Baylor's phone rang. It was the chairman on the line, and he was still another ten minutes out. We sipped our coffee and waited.

The chairman, Todd, walked in, and Baylor waved at him. We shook hands and exchanged greetings and then he excused himself to get his own coffee. By appearances, Todd was not what I expected from a chairman or a businessman. He was wearing what looked like a track suit and came off as a thirtysomething who had just come from the gym. I'm pretty sure I was right. Todd sat down and we started off the discussion with who I was and some of the standard stuff I had done in my videotaping. Baylor and Mark had coached me about staying on message and succinct.

None of this seemed to make a difference in Todd's demeanor or expression. He gave the impression that the meeting was just another formality and he had other things to do. We probed him a bit on his county and what was going on.

In most elections, each county in the district would hold a meeting where every member of the party's "board" would come together and each candidate would get a chance to speak and sometimes answer some questions. Then, the board members would vote on who they were going to endorse publicly. This endorsement would be publicized, usually in a press release and also a voter's guide that laid out who Republicans should vote for. It was hard to tell how often or how well an endorsement worked, but it was certainly valuable. Without the endorsement, it was a tougher battle, since many voters would follow this guide, particularly if they didn't really do their own research by reading up and meeting candidates. On the other hand, this was an election cycle that started seeing voters become more independent and less trustful of politicians, including those who ran the local county party.

Todd told us some of what we already knew. Butler County had held their meeting and attempted to endorse a candidate based on their rules. The rules are different in every county, but Butler's were essentially multiple rounds of voting where the lowest vote-getter is dropped in each round and continues until one candidate reaches a certain threshold, which is usually 60 to 80 percent. In some cases, the final round may not get any candidate to that threshold, which results in no endorsement. Todd told us the story of their meeting about a month ago, just before I entered the race (and, oddly, before the filing requirement for candidates), when they were unable to reach the threshold for endorsement.

We asked whether they would try again or not, and Todd said it wasn't likely. We exchanged a few more comments, and Todd said he had to go to work (in a track suit?) and needed to leave. We shook hands, and he left. Baylor and I went out to the parking lot and chatted a bit. Our reactions were the same: "What the hell was that?!" We chatted a few more minutes, and I headed to my office to catch up on some of my own work. We would talk later that day, probably several times, as we often did.

Most of the other county chairman meetings were similar. Some of the chairmen were more interested in hearing who I was and what issues were important to me. Some were more interested in telling me about themselves. And still others were going through the motions and polite but didn't show any real interest. I learned why the latter group wasn't necessarily showing a lot of interest later that day.

When Baylor and I did talk again, he had interesting news. Since the time to file for candidacy was almost a month old, he had found out who else was running and did a little preliminary digging on their background. Seventeen people had filed as candidates. As discussed previously, Roger Reynolds, the previous front runner and Boehner's favorite, had already dropped out, and an additional filing had been dismissed as incomplete.

But I was still shocked by the number of candidates. I had thought there would be several candidates, maybe even six or seven, especially for an open primary since the incumbent was not running. But I never would have thought there would be *seventeen*. Baylor ran down the list with what little he had pieced together so far. He admitted that not all his information was verified, but it was what he knew at the time.

The list looked like this:

CANDIDATE	AGE	OCCUPATION	PREVIOUS POLITICAL EXPERIENCE
Matt Ashworth	48	Local business employee	None
Bill Beagle	51	State senator	State senator for six years
Warren Davidson	46	Local business owner	Former township trustee
Tim Derickson	55	State representative	Trustee and representative for seventeen years
Scott George	48	Consultant	None
Eric Haemmerle	43	Teacher	None
Terri King	55	Attorney	Ran and lost for judge and state representative
Joe Matvey	55	Local business employee	None
Ed Meer	39	Local factory worker	None
John Robbins	77	Retired factory worker	None
Jim Spurlino	52	Local business owner	None
Michael Smith	44	Unemployed banker	None
Kevin White	51	Pilot, U.S. Air Force veteran	None
J.D. Winteregg	33	Local farm employee	Ran against Boehner in 2014 primary
George Wooley	61	Local business employee	Former Republican precinct chair

The Other Candidates

I spent a lot of time with the other candidates at events and forums where we were all invited. We would inevitably spend time backstage, waiting our turn, chatting, etc. Some conversations were just social and perfunctory and others were of more substance, even occasionally talking about other candidates or issues. Very few were personal, open, and honest. Like we were part of a club of performers hired to do the same job. It was a bond of sorts, destined to be short-lived, but a unique bond because of what we were all doing at the time.

Bill Beagle was typical of my opponents who were holding an elected office. He was smart enough, motivated enough, and had a following that wanted him to win. Term limits in Ohio meant that he needed to find his next gig after serving as senator, and Boehner resigning may have meant he had that. Mike Turner, a then-current U.S. congressman in an adjacent district, called Beagle shortly after Boehner resigned.

Beagle later shared with me that Turner told him he should run for the seat and that he'd win it. These and many other of the same type of conversations led Beagle to run. It was the next logical step when this once-in-a-lifetime opportunity presented itself.

Beagle made two trips to DC and found more encouragement. A report prepared by a political consulting firm helped. One of the key passages said, "The bottom line is that based on our analysis, Beagle can clearly win this race, and unlike all of the other potential opponents, he possesses many paths to victory." Beagle was indeed encouraged and started contacting his friends in the political world. They all agreed that announcing early, maybe even being the first to do so, might keep others from getting in the race. He was the first to announce his candidacy, and had he raised enough money, the seat should've been his.

He is a nice guy, and he's smart. He was the only one of my opponents I identified with throughout the campaign. His problem was similar to mine . . . only worse. He wouldn't throw bombshells. He never made a statement that the press deemed newsworthy. In fact, he would have been a credible, hardworking congressman, but he lacked the ability, or more likely the nature, to get elected. He was unwilling to criticize his opponents and reluctant to stray from conventional Republican thinking. More importantly, he never found the resources needed to raise the money. He was a "nice guys finish last" kind of guy.

I did not know Tim Derickson before the campaign, and I never got to know him, so my opinions here were gathered from afar. However, my strong impression was that he was an even *nicer* guy than Bill Beagle. A genuinely likeable guy—albeit one who would be eaten alive by the Washington swamp. And I mean that as a compliment, not a criticism. But I also don't think he would have been able to do much in DC if he was elected.

J.D. Winteregg had run against Boehner in the 2014 primary. Boehner won with 72 percent of the vote (a relatively low figure for a sitting speaker, but that didn't reflect any great enthusiasm for Winteregg). Interestingly, Winteregg received far fewer votes in the campaign year I ran than he received just two years before against Boehner. His campaign that prior cycle was noted for his commercials touting "Electile Dysfunction," which tried to take a shot at Boehner. It not only failed to make a dent in the primary, but it was also widely reported to have cost him his job as a professor at a local college.

Winteregg was a nice and affable guy, but he seemed to be running on the fact that he challenged Boehner before instead of waiting for the open seat like the rest of us in 2016. He also liked to point out that he could relate to a younger crowd, as he was the youngest among us Republican candidates at age thirty-three. Otherwise, his positions were mostly in line with the rest of us.

Scott George was a businessman with a history of working at Procter & Gamble as well as a consultant. He was probably the most like me and seemed to have the same take on many issues. My early guess was that he would be a formidable opponent, but he never gained traction nor raised any money to speak of.

Kevin White was a United Airlines pilot who had an extensive military career, including combat missions. He attended almost all the campaign events and was a little quirky at times. He prided himself in telling audiences he was the only one who had policy details on his website, including tax reforms. I never got to ask him if the Congressional Budget Office got around to scoring it. (The CBO is designated by Congress to provide official cost estimates for proposed legislation.) He also said to more than one opponent that he won every debate he was in and was agitated when the media failed to recognize him as a top-tier candidate.

Warren Davidson joined the U.S. Army after graduating high school and eventually continued his education at West Point. Following his graduation from there, he continued in the army as an Army Ranger. After twelve years in the army, he left and returned to work in his father's tool and die business within the Eighth Congressional District. During this time, he also earned an MBA from Notre Dame and eventually purchased the business from his father.

There was also one Democrat running. He was a recent graduate of college named Corey Foister. He was twenty-five years old and had no political experience. Baylor had heard the Democrats had difficulty finding anyone to run in this district since it was a foregone conclusion they would lose. No one knew Foister's background, except it appeared he was drafted for this suicide mission.

There was also a Green Party candidate named Jim Condit Jr. He had run for numerous other offices under the Constitution Party, which is a far-right party, so it was odd that he was running as a Green, which typically takes far left positions. Baylor said he heard some odd stories about him but felt it didn't matter since his chances of winning were about the same as Foister's.

Interestingly, Baylor was getting a few calls about me. Other campaigns had done just the same as Baylor and had looked into who was running. Now, Baylor was getting calls from some people around the district asking who I was, where I came from, and how much money I might be able to raise. I was getting a lot of notice amongst our competitors. While this was nice and even a little encouraging, the attention was not from voters, and I tried to ignore this bit of notice and notoriety. It just wasn't meaningful. The campaign was about to really get started, and I needed to focus on getting people to know me and vote for me.

CHAPTER 12

Meetings with Interest Groups

BAYLOR RECEIVED A CALL FROM a staff member of American Israel Public Affairs Committee (AIPAC) in mid-January. Their official mission is "to encourage and persuade the U.S. government to enact specific policies that create a strong, enduring, and mutually beneficial relationship with our ally Israel."[10] They further state that they "engage with and educate decision-makers about the bonds that unite the two countries, and how it is in America's best interest to strengthen those bonds and help ensure that the Jewish state remains safe, strong, and secure." The staffer wanted to meet with me, discuss issues that were important to AIPAC, and elicit a position from me about Israel.

I was a little surprised that Israel would be a campaign issue. While I wasn't uninterested in AIPAC's positions and discussions about Israel, the district's voters seemed to be more interested in other issues. Mark and Baylor had been pushing me to talk about reliably conservative issues such as guns, abortion, immigration, etc. Israel seemed like many other issues I *wanted* to speak on but was implicitly discouraged from discussing.

Baylor assured me that AIPAC was influential and that it was important to meet with them. He explained that the group was interested in every congressman's position and, being the former speaker's district, they would definitely want to meet and discuss my positions. I happily agreed.

Before the meeting, I brushed up on Israel, and Baylor gave me some highlights of what would likely come up. He also showed me the Israel-focused position papers of a few other congressmen and asked me to consider whether I would commit to publishing something similar. As I read through them, nothing stuck out as anything but logical and reasonable.

As was our custom for meetings like this, it was held in a coffee shop, about mid-morning. Marc Ashed, the Midwest deputy political director, walked in and waved to Baylor. He was youngish, probably mid-thirties, and well dressed. He looked professional and was well spoken. We exchanged short pleasantries and then got down to business. He began by gauging my knowledge of Israel and then my positions on specific issues. His questions were centered on what you might expect for the mid-2010s, including foreign aid from the United States ($3.1 billion at that time[11]), threats from Syria and Palestine, and the location of the U.S. embassy, among other issues. I think my answers assured him my positions would align with continuing a close relationship with Israel and current foreign aid levels. After passing the knowledge test part of this meeting, we spent the better part of an hour discussing almost all of AIPAC's positions in some detail. I also was asked to consider issuing a position paper to detail my support. In the end, I got a smile, a hearty handshake, and an invitation to AIPAC's Cincinnati Annual Event. This would be a full cocktail and dinner affair with multiple speakers. I told him we would check my schedule and get back to him.

Baylor and I huddled after Ashed left and discussed issuing a position paper. I told him I had absolutely no problem doing so and would welcome it, then I asked Baylor to explain what effect he believed a published position paper would have on the campaign. Baylor said there would not be an endorsement and likely no donations (the same could be said for many other advocacy groups). However, the position paper would please AIPAC, as well as those voters in the district who support Israel, so it could translate to some votes. He added that going to the event would be a big plus, as he anticipated most—if not all—other candidates would not attend.

"Let's go then," I decided. "Sign up me, Tricia, and you. I think it will be interesting and I want to put out a position paper too. This is a no-brainer to me." And with that, I officially became a supporter of AIPAC and Israel.

Over the next few weeks, Baylor and I worked on the position paper so it could be released before the event. In the end, here is what we came up with:

Introduction

A few years ago, I missed the opportunity to visit Israel with a group of fellow community leaders from the Cincinnati United Way. It was unfortunate, but my business required I stay in southwestern Ohio. In my decades of charitable involvement, I worked alongside many wonderful members of the Jewish community. Together, we endeavor to solve some of society's most complex problems, particularly through the prism of early childhood intervention. It's been a privilege and I've enjoyed learning about the rich Jewish culture through their personal experiences. Fortitude and accomplishment are among the most consistent traits, for which I have much respect. I know through these individuals that these traits are alive and well in Israel. Moreover, I realize Israel's critical role for democracy in the Middle East. Their unwavering commitment to freedom and individual liberty must be supported by the United States at all levels.

Security Threats

We are laser-focused on the serious security threat Iran poses to our way of life. I will continue to speak loudly against the disastrous U.S.–Iranian deal. It emboldens our enemies across the world and it was a sad decision by feckless leaders. More recently, I was outraged when U.S. Secretary of State John Kerry said he is "sure" that money from the deal will go to terrorists who want to kill Americans and the people of Israel. I'll fight to undo the damage from this deal and halt the flow of monetary assets to the Iranian government. Sanctions were working well and we must not be deceived by phony platitudes of peace from those who have chanted "death to America" for more than four decades.

For far too long, Hamas and Hezbollah have gone unchecked. If elected, I would support Israeli-led efforts to disarm and defeat those radical terrorist organizations. Through my voting power, I would support financial aid for security assistance and increase annual amounts Congress plans to take up this year. Due to the nature of this special election, the winner will take office in June and this vote could be crucial to delivering this much-needed aid. I'd be proud to do it.

Conclusion

As a businessman, I never cared much for political rhetoric. I prefer action. If elected, I will go to Washington as a strong supporter of the special relationship between the U.S. and Israel. It's that simple.

I was quite pleased with the way it turned out. It also seemed to please the folks at AIPAC, which was not the sole intent but was good to hear. Several weeks later, we attended the Cincinnati Annual Event, and, as Baylor predicted, I was the only candidate there. There were about 500 people present, with only a few elected officials. We spent the time before and after dinner and the speakers talking to many of the other attendees. Everyone we talked to seemed happy I had attended and was glad to hear of my support for Israel. Mission accomplished.

We had meetings with many other groups that had specific interests as well. As was indicative of the day, there were Tea Party groups in most of the counties, and we would meet with each of them. Some were coffee-shop meetings, and others were in the home of a member of the group. These meetings tended to focus on fiscal matters such as the federal debt and diving into whether I was truly conservative enough for them. They also would address other issues such as property rights, universal health care, and other perceived intrusions into our freedoms.

At one such meeting, I would meet a competitor, Warren Davidson, for the first time. Baylor and I were in a coffee shop with several ladies of one such Tea Party group. About halfway into our conversation, Davidson walked in by himself and sat down. One of the ladies remarked who he was and waved him over. I remember thinking that he couldn't be a serious contender because he just didn't look or act like it. He was dressed in a suit but no tie and was wearing the kind of black work shoes you see on fast-food workers. He also had a backpack. Just not a particularly professional look and kind of disheveled. He said very little and then went back to his table across the room.

I occasionally would glance his way to see who he might be meeting with but no one ever showed up. Thirty minutes later, he got up and walked out alone, just as he had come in. When our meeting was over, Baylor and I walked out and remarked how odd that was and his awkward demeanor. Neither of us gave him another thought as a serious threat.

Besides meeting with groups in person, we also were periodically busy filling out questionnaires from various groups. Baylor and Mark explained that we should respond to every one, regardless of where they came from. To not do so would cause more notice and possibly be regarded as a slight to the group.

All of these questionnaires were structured to get at the issue or cause that the group cared about most. The ones from the National Rifle Association (NRA) and right-to-life groups were the most obvious examples of this. Most would have endless questions asking the same thing several different ways. Generally, Mark or Baylor would go through them and suggest answers and then send them to me for approval or edits. It really was just a "check the box" exercise, since most could have read my website and gotten the same thing. After we sent these questionnaires back, we would wait for a week or two while they graded you and then some would issue a rating or approval. It seemed like a bit of nonsense to me most of the time.

CHAPTER 13

The Futility of Candidate Forums

THE VISION I'D ALWAYS HAD of campaigning was about to be realized. I had my first event scheduled in a few days at Eaton High School in Preble County. I was excited to finally start talking about issues and why I would be the best Republican nominee, as well as a great congressman.

To prepare for this event, and all the ones that followed, Mark and Baylor laid out what they thought I should say and how to react to a variety of possible questions. We worked largely from the script used at the video shoot. Mark explained that my message had to be consistent and should remain almost the same for every event. He said, "There will be a lot of these, and the audience will be different every night, so we want to hone your message, emphasize your talking points, and make sure the takeaway is the same every time. If we are all over the place, nothing is memorable. We need to just keep hitting the big ones. You've never run for political office. You're tired of Washington and career politicians. You have true conservative values. That's it."

Then he kind of laid a bombshell on me. I had always thought these events—debates, candidate forums, meet and greets, etc.— were the most important part of a campaign. You get to meet the candidates. Talk about issues. Answer questions. Show your intelligence and grasp of the issues. "Not so," Mark told me. "These forums don't matter. You won't win an election based on your performance at these things. The only thing that matters is that you show up and don't screw up. There is only downside. Stay on message, don't get rattled or off script, and you'll be fine."

I trusted Mark but was shocked that these events wouldn't make a difference. I thought I *could* make a difference standing among my competition and showing my thorough knowledge and ideas. I also knew I was a natural public speaker. Not flashy. No Tony Robbins. But I was confident and had given enough speeches to feel comfortable, which I thought would show through. I believed Mark but thought in my own mind that I'd show him and go out and kill it.

Political campaign events where multiple candidates show up are typically labeled as "debates," but they're not. A debate would be where an issue is raised and candidates take turns discussing it and offering points and counterpoints. There is back and forth. One person may raise an issue that the other must respond to.

This does not happen. Not anywhere in campaigning. Even televised presidential "debates" barely take that form. It often comes down to answering the question with your canned answer. It's a Q&A at best. More accurately, it's a precise preformed question followed by a rote answer.

The other interesting thing is that the format for these events—let's call them "forums"—is designed for brevity. That may be because of the short attention span of audiences. Or maybe the issue that the candidates have short attention spans. Or both. But in this race, brevity was needed because of the large number of candidates who were likely to attend.

In a typical forum, candidates answered questions based on alphabetical order or how we happened to be seated. If a forum was thoughtful, the sponsors might randomly assign the sequence of candidates, or go in reverse for every other question. Every once in a while, there were not assigned seats, and it was up to the candidates to seat ourselves. Of course, some of us assumed the seating arrangement would affect the order in which we would speak. I found the jockeying for seats entertaining (as the audiences probably did as well) but also somewhat nerve-racking.

Each forum started with a brief statement (thirty to sixty seconds) from the candidates, focused on what distinguished them from everyone else in the race. Sometimes, if organizers were generous, we might've gotten two minutes, but this was rare. Then we moved on to the Q&A portion. Candidate responses were almost always capped at thirty to forty-five seconds. It was not nearly enough time. Imagine having a reasonable amount of knowledge on a complex issue like immigration or national security or the federal budget and getting *thirty seconds* to give your thoughts on it. It was mostly ridiculous and often led me to see the wisdom of Mark's assertion that these things don't matter. In most cases, it would only show the few candidates that were unprepared or lacked knowledge on the subject.

Regarding response order, first was always good and usually best. The middle provided extra time to think. The last person, especially when most of the candidates showed up, usually had almost nothing to add. When a dozen conservative people have given their position on the federal budget, there is almost never anything new to add by the end.

I was excited to attend my first forum. I'd never spoken about politics before a crowd, and I was looking forward to sizing myself up against my competitors. Tricia and Baylor rode with me to an event hall a bit out in the country. Along the way, we talked about what to expect, and Baylor gave his list of dos and don'ts. It was all pretty logical and basic stuff, but it was good to be reminded. He shared things like "stand up straight," "listen carefully to the questions," "speak clearly," "emphasize important points," "make eye contact," and "don't worry about what the competitors say," among several others. Tricia chimed in with "and smile." She knew my penchant for being all business, at times to my detriment.

Like we would for every forum after this, we arrived a little early and sat in the car for a few minutes. Everyone made sure every hair was in place and we had no food in our teeth. Then, at Tricia's suggestion, we held hands and prayed. Tricia is great at leading prayer. She always says the right things, and in this moment she lifted my spirits and passed a calm and confident air around the car. Amen. Because we were early, we had time to socialize a bit and get the lay of the land before the event began. Where the candidates were to be seated as well as the moderator was Baylor's responsibility. He'd also talk to the host and then generally was chatting a bit with the other campaign managers and political operatives attending. Most importantly, he would be on the lookout for press and make sure he talked to them. Periodically, he'd check back with me and give me some scoop on what he heard or who he talked to. I think he was also checking my appearance and generally making sure I was okay and ready to go.

Tricia, who was usually the most sociable in the room (and every room I've ever seen her in), talked with anyone and everyone. She stayed near me at the beginning, but eventually she was off in a conversation with someone she just met. Then, she'd wave me over for an introduction. I was used to it, but it was kind of funny to watch her work a room way better than her husband . . . who was a candidate.

Although I am definitely an introvert, I've acquired the skill of appearing otherwise. However, it does take me quite a bit of effort. Throughout the campaign process, there were times I was successful in working a room and chatting up folks I'd never met, but it was never natural for me. Sometimes I'd be good for a while, then I'd revert to being comfortable not talking to anyone. It was a constant and conscious effort for me to start and maintain conversations. However, I had realized that was my job once I entered the race. I tried hard in this first event, and think I won over most and they thought of me as a nonintrovert.

Members of the audience continued to funnel into the hall for the next twenty minutes. They did not fit any discernible type of person or voter. Most looked like they came from work. Some had on flannel shirts, and some had on suits, and there were a whole lot of people who appeared in between. Some had bewildered looks, and some looked like they showed up for a dentist appointment. After about twenty minutes, the moderators announced that the event was beginning in five minutes and everyone should be seated. The candidates were asked to find their seats on the stage.

I didn't count that night, but Baylor told me later seven candidates were present. I thought the low number was odd at the time—there were seventeen candidates running—but over the weeks ahead, it became apparent that some candidates only went to forums near their homes, and others almost never went at all. I never knew whether some didn't get invited or were simply unaware of some forums, but it was evident early on that only six of us would attend almost every event. It was Bill Beagle and Tim Derickson, the two current politicians; J. D. Winteregg, the former primary opponent of Boehner; Warren Davidson, the other businessman; Kevin White, the pilot; and me. All but White had campaign staff.

The moderator, a local Republican Party official, announced the format and got us started. Opening remarks were first and we were allowed sixty seconds each. We'd go in the order we were seated, and he assured us and the audience that the seating assignments were chosen randomly. Over time, I began to wonder whether the arrangements were truly random. Depending on where we were, it seemed like the order usually favored the hometown candidate, though I'm not sure it mattered. I was just glad not to go first on my first night. It was good to observe a few first.

The candidates who were current politicians delivered very smooth and well-rehearsed opening remarks. They emphasized their experience in political office and how they'd get things done in Washington, just like they had here at home. There was an air of confidence, but neither of them had a lot of charisma and seemed somewhat flat. A couple other candidates went, then I was up. The microphone was passed to me, and I stood up and delivered my sixty-second speech, the same one I would use, sometimes shortened or lengthened a bit, for every forum thereafter. It went something like this:

> *Hi. I'm Jim Spurlino and I'm not a professional politician. In fact, I've never run for office. I'm a husband, father, and small business owner. And I'm worried what professional politicians*

are doing to our country. *Their greed and political games are hurting us. When John Boehner resigned, I watched as they lined up to advance their careers. And I waited, hoping to see if someone who could lead would run. But no one did. Just the same old politicians.*

So I decided to step aside from my business and run for Congress. I've lived in this area all my life, and I employ more than one hundred people in Middletown. I do business all across this district. No one knows this area better than I do.

I started at the bottom, learned every job, and eventually started my own business. What I've seen lately is that Congress is made up of a bunch of lawyers, government staffers, and professional politicians. None of which have worked construction sites, built a business, or met a payroll every week.

Not one of them look out for everyday men and women trying to make a living and provide for their families.

Professional politicians have chipped away at our national foundation. They move to Washington, and they become Washington—all to advance their own careers.

In fact, a congressman from Michigan got re-elected for the twenty-seventh time last election. Our country's founders designed a limited government. They were patriotic and wanted to do public service, not make it a career or get a big raise.

Elect me to Congress, and I'll work in Washington. But I won't become Washington.

My home, family, and business will stay right here.

Want to know more about me? Here's a few things to consider: I'm a conservative Republican in the mold of Ronald Reagan. I'm pro-life and do not support federal funds for abortions.

I'm a gun owner and strong supporter of gun rights and have a CCW.

*Obamacare is a disaster. We need **patient-centered** and market-based solutions, not an expansion of Medicaid.*

*We are all taxed too much. We need to **tax** less and **spend** less, and I support a simplified tax system.*

Seven years of Barack Obama has created a country we don't recognize anymore.

Go to VoteSpurlino.com to find out more. I'm Jim Spurlino. I'm not a professional politician. I'm a conservative Republican. And I ask for your support.

Thank you.

It flowed naturally, as I had rehearsed it many times. I hit the bolded terms with extra emphasis, as Mark coached me to. I tried to use some hand gestures and scan the crowd, looking back and forth. Every so often, I would see a nodding head or a clear look of approval. Mostly, there seemed to be a lot of stone faces in the audience. People paying attention but not providing much of a response or feedback of any sort. At least once every forum, Tricia would come into my view. She was always smiling and wide-eyed, silently cheering me on. Seeing her always made me pick up my voice inflection and volume a bit.

I finished and sat down and found Tricia again. She had the same smiling face I'd seen just moments before, and it made me smile in return. Then I stopped smiling, fearful that I accidently smiled during the next candidate's opening remarks and who knows how that would be interpreted! The opening remarks finished up, and we went on to questions, for which candidates were allotted thirty seconds to answer.

To prepare for the event, I had rehearsed answers to all the obvious questions. The moderator did not disappoint and hit all the big issues. We went through guns and immigration, health care and education, and so on. There weren't any questions that were a surprise, and there weren't vast differences in positions between candidates in how they answered. There were some nuances, but nothing substantive.

Positions on gun control were typical of this. The most extreme position was: "There are already too many gun laws, and we need to repeal every one of them. No gun laws are the best gun laws." The most nuanced position may have been mine, which was still further to the right than I was comfortable with. It was along the lines of: "The Second Amendment should not be repealed, and we should fight to retain our right to protect our families and property."

I was a little disappointed that there were no surprises or fireworks during the forum. It felt like we all lined up and sang from pretty much the same hymnal. Following the end of the forum, the candidates shook hands with each other, and we all made it down the stairs of the stage and into an audience that seemed mostly intent on getting to their cars. I spoke with all audience members who were interested and had the time, and I stayed until no one was left who wanted to talk. In this case, about a dozen or so came up with well wishes and a few had follow-up questions of some sort. After finishing the last conversation, Tricia and I walked out into the night and found our car for the drive home. Whether Mark said it mattered or not, we both thought it went great and had an impact on many of those who attended.

CHAPTER 14

The Money Hunt Continues

SOON AFTER THE CAMPAIGN BEGAN, days—and entire weeks—became a blur. I rarely looked ahead more than a day or two on the calendars Baylor prepared and then constantly revised. Whenever possible, I would retreat to my office and run my business. It was familiar and safe. It also gave me reprieves from the constant nagging to raise additional funds for the campaign. There was rarely a day that went by where I didn't get "the question" from Mark or Baylor: "How much did you raise today?"

I always had a list of people to call. The list was comprised of people I knew and others who Mark and Baylor had identified as potential donors, based on having contributed to other candidates in the past. It was all public information, although I'm not sure how they got it. Most of these would be pure cold calls, and I did not enjoy them. More than once, I would be halfway through my opening spiel, only to be interrupted and asked, "How'd you get my number?" Not a good start.

Typically, I would set aside an hour and make some calls at the office in the morning, then I'd continue for about two hours or so in the afternoon. I found asking people for money to be unpleasant and uncomfortable. Mark would encourage me with small scripts and advice. It was always for "the cause" or "help send me to Congress where I'll make a difference for the issues we care about." I rarely had this much trouble making calls to raise money for charities, but that was for someone else and always those less fortunate. This just felt different.

When calling people I knew, I could at least connect with them on things we had in common. I'd usually start by catching up on each other's work and family and then explain, if they didn't know, that I was running for Congress and needed a donation. Most were still on the phone after I asked for money, and they usually said they would help. In many cases, it was a surprise what they would end up sending after the call. Eventually, Mark taught me to make a specific request that I believed was at the high end of whatever I thought was possible for them. This set me up for disappointment a little too often, but there were some nice surprises the other way once in a while.

One of my business's best customers was Baker Concrete, and the founders, Dan and Cindy Baker, were personal friends of ours as well. One day when I was in the Baker Concrete office, I stuck my head in Cindy's office to say hello. She was always one of the nicest people I knew in the industry, but she is also a smart and tough businessperson. We chatted for a bit about business and then she asked, without my prompting, about giving to my campaign. Although I felt a sheepish about it, I went through the rules about maximum contributions from individuals. On her office whiteboard, I laid out that there were actually two elections to be held for Boehner's seat. One was to finish his current term after the general election and the other for the next full term. This meant that she could actually double the amount of the maximum for this primary. After I was done, she repeated what I had laid out and thanked me for the information. I never thought about asking her for a specific amount. I was just thankful for the interest and how supportive she had always been of me professionally.

A few weeks later, Baylor called to tell me that we'd received Cindy's check for the (double) maximum amount and the same from her husband, Dan. That was $2,700 × 4 for a total of $10,800. This was a huge boost. After speaking with Cindy, I was hopeful she'd contribute, but I never really knew what would happen until the check arrived in those situations. I picked up my phone and immediately called to thank them. It was one of many shots of confidence I would receive unexpectedly throughout the campaign.

I received seventeen "max-out" donations and almost all of them came from my industry contacts. CEOs and owners from across the country had made very generous donations and usually without my personal ask. There were also some other surprises that would come with Baylor's donation summary calls. The owner of an HVAC contracting company in Missouri gave $500. I'd never met him, but he saw some of the media coverage in *USA Today* and sent a check. We received checks from a few well-known supporters of the Democratic Party in the area. It seemed that supporting their favorite Republican was an acknowledgement that a Democrat would not win. A retired Cincinnati judge sent a check for $100. As far as I remember, I never appeared before him. And one of my favorites, a five-dollar anonymous donation. I guess they wanted to help but weren't too proud about it.

There were also some PAC donations. Mostly, these came from corporate PACs or association PACs in my industry. The maximum for a PAC was $5,000, and several gave that amount. While these were healthy amounts, they did not compare to the Super PAC spending that was underway (there were no limits on what Super PACs could spend). Mark had been getting intel that some Super PACs were starting to spend money about sixty days out from the election. The amounts were quite large.

The Club for Growth was one of these Super PACs. They spent $1,133,765 supporting Davidson, which I will discuss in more detail later. Another Super PAC, called Defending Main Street, spent $280,536 on him.[12] The Right Way Initiative spent $703,489 for Derickson. Along with $250,000 spent by the Credit Union National Association PAC for Derickson, his outside money total approached Davidson's.[13] No one else in the race was even registering any outside money support, and it was starting to show. The amount of TV/radio airtime was a pretty good indicator of whose bank account had ballooned recently.

Meanwhile, my biggest funder—me—was not so anxious to give any additional funds. While I thought I would've been raising more money by that time in the campaign, it simply wasn't happening. When I started, I had committed to a minimum level of spending that I knew I could and would fund. Mark had explained this could be set up as a loan and then repaid as donations came in. He also said that people would ask if I put any of my own money in the campaign and the answer could influence their own donations. By this point in the campaign, I had invested $150,000 but had capped the total at $200,000. A month before the election, Mark started asking about the last $50,000 and whether there might be any more behind it.

I was adamant about there not being any more. I knew the amounts flowing into Davidson and Derickson were dwarfing anything we were likely to raise, and I couldn't see how an extra $50,000 to $100,000 would make a difference. To that end, I was unsure why Mark was urging me to consider it. It may have been in an effort to do as well as we could, but at the time I didn't see any logic to his request. Looking back on the situation now, I will give Mark credit for seeing the need for a big donation or the kind of spending Davidson and Derickson were making to be a major contender. He pressed me about whether my Super PAC was going to raise that or not, and it was clear he saw the magnitude of the fight.

My last hope was local fundraising at events being spearheaded by industry leaders. A regional contracting association sponsored such a fundraising event. Its CEO, John Morris, arranged for it to be held in one of their larger spaces, and it included some of the area's contracting company executives along with other members of the association, such as legal and accounting firms. It was a nice event and had about twenty attendees, and all of them donated. I appreciated it very much, but it was not going to change the trajectory of the race.

A customer of mine, Jim Jurgensen Jr., organized another event. Jim was a friend—I had known him for about a decade, and I had known his father even longer. Jim Jr. worked hard to round up attendees for an event at a local hotel. We had a large ballroom set up with drinks and hors d'oeuvres. Again, about twenty or so folks showed up and all contributed to my campaign. My favorite part of the night was seeing Jim Sr., who flew in from Florida for the event. That meant a lot to me.

I greatly appreciated the hard work by John and Jim to organize both events. However, like I had experienced in other parts of this campaign, there didn't seem to be much interest in primary politics beyond those who are regularly involved in such things. It was also clear that my late entry into the race had not really given us enough time to develop these events, nor make the case for my candidacy adequately ahead of such events. Nothing could be done to change this now.

While we were not meeting our fundraising goals, Tricia pressed for spending on yard signs, T-shirts, buttons, and stickers (as she had been doing since early in the campaign). Mark said none of these make a big enough difference, and we should be spending our money elsewhere. He emphasized that campaigns flush with cash would spend on paraphernalia and billboards. This was clearly not our problem.

Tricia kept up the pressure and was unhappy because the other campaigns had signs. She was very competitive. Mark finally relented a little and ordered some yard signs along with a several large ones for major roads and intersections. When they arrived, Tricia and the volunteer staff were very pleased, but Mark would not relent on T-shirts and buttons. So Tricia, as she has been known to do, decided she was done asking and ordered them herself. Within a week, we had T-shirts for the volunteers, and she was making the buttons from office store supplies and printed stickers. I was happy for her to put her energy into an aspect of the campaign she was personally passionate about, and it was nice to see the signs too.

Mark was on a never-ending quest to help find donors and voters. One day, he called me with an idea. He mentioned a young attorney in Cincinnati whom he had worked with in the past and who he thought would be worth meeting. "He's a sharp kid and works for one of the largest law firms in the region," said Mark. "A big plus is that his wife is the daughter of the CEO of one of Cincinnati's largest firms. They're kind of an up-and-coming power couple." He went on and told me that he would put us in contact with each other, then it would be up to me to see where it goes.

I knew of the law firm and of the wife's father, and I was definitely intrigued. Mark sent over a mutual introduction email to both of us, and a few days later we were emailing about meeting soon. We finally decided on a nice restaurant north of Cincinnati. It was convenient for both of us and had enough dining rooms that we could find a quiet table. We also decided to invite our wives.

It was a Wednesday, and we had no campaign events planned. This was a rare semi-night off that Tricia and I looked forward to even if we were meeting strangers. We arrived and they were already seated in a private corner of the restaurant. We introduced ourselves and sat down. They were a nice couple and easy to talk to. They were youngish, probably midthirties. They told us he had worked for this law firm since law school and practiced general business law, and she worked for a company downtown.

The conversation flowed effortlessly, and they seemed genuinely interested in my race and helping out. By the end of the evening, it seemed like they had a lot of ideas on how they might help and were anxious to start. He said he would be in touch very soon, and she promised to start working her contacts. We left the evening feeling like we had just met friends we had known for some time and looked forward to staying in touch. There was even talk of when we would meet next for dinner.

We exchanged a few emails over the next two weeks. He was busy but still working on ideas to assist with fundraising and introductions. Following the emails, he set up a call, saying he wanted to discuss some things. When we did talk, he was as energetic and supportive as ever. He said he wanted to set up a time for me to come to his office and meet all the attorneys. This would be great since they had over 100 attorneys in his office and over 500 throughout the firm. He also said he had spoken to his managing partner who wanted me to go with him to a local high school basketball game that Friday where he would introduce me to several additional contacts. The high school he mentioned was the largest in the district, and Saturday high school basketball was very popular there. I was excited about both opportunities.

Later that week, he emailed and canceled the basketball game. He didn't give a reason but said he would reschedule. He also didn't mention the office visit. I didn't think much of it. I thanked him and told him I'd look forward to hearing back when they were able to schedule both.

A couple of more weeks passed and there was no word, so I emailed him. I received no answer to the email for a few days, so I texted him on his cell. He didn't respond for a few days, so I called him. After he didn't pick up, I left a voicemail. After a few more days, I sent Mark an email with an update on everything since he had been asking. I briefly explained what we'd talked about. I specifically said that I wasn't asking Mark to call since it seemed childish to do so. I never received a call, text, or email from him, and Mark never heard a word either.

Well after the election, out of curiosity, I did a little forensic work to see if I could figure out what happened. With many law firms, certain issues will get emailed around for approval by partners. Or in many cases, something may get emailed around for blackballing (i.e., when a partner may weigh in and say, "No, let's not do that," or "I have a problem with that."). In my case, apparently there was some discussion about whether to support or endorse me that came up when the office meeting and basketball game ideas got discussed.

As I heard the story, I remembered that there was a partner in that office who once represented someone who had sued me over a business matter. The claim made was for damages in the millions. This partner had thought they were going to win a huge sum from me. The lawsuit dragged on for two years and finally went to trial. When this partner, who represented the plaintiff, had finished putting on his case, my attorney made a motion to dismiss the case. The judge ruled almost entirely in our favor, leaving them with a shell of a case. We started our defense and counterclaim and were clearly making great strides in front of the jury when they decided to scramble for a settlement. The case was quickly settled in 2010. It was an embarrassment for the partner and his client, as I got everything I wanted from the settlement, with a pittance to them.

The real explanation of the young lawyer ghosting me was never shared with me firsthand, but I heard enough from others to realize his partner still had his feelings hurt since I never missed the opportunity to talk about his performance in the lawsuit. It was a small lesson for me to be a better winner, but over the years I had seen enough frivolous lawsuits that I became outspoken about lawyers taking cases they shouldn't just to earn fees. In this case, it was several hundred thousand dollars paid to the plaintiffs' attorneys plus consultants that charged almost half that. In any case, you would think the young lawyer would have responded in some way. He could've just called and told me that his assistance wasn't possible any longer, but I guess being professional and courteous isn't a value for everyone.

CHAPTER 15

The Grind: Door Knocks, My Call Center, and a Bake Sale

"DOOR KNOCKS" IS SHORTHAND FOR candidates going door-to-door and talking to voters. (It's one of those terms used by insiders.) Years ago, it was a traditional form of campaigning—before TV and radio became commonplace and certainly before social media—but it is still used today.

I hadn't thought much about walking around neighborhoods and knocking on doors, but Mark and Baylor made it clear that I would be doing that every weekend until the election. This was despite Mark making it clear that candidate forums and door knocks would not make a difference, at least not like money would. The door-knock strategy included not just me but any volunteers whom I could recruit.

Mostly with the help of Tricia, who was much more persuasive than me, we began to ask friends if they would help. The idea was that we would meet somewhere on Saturday and Sunday mornings (typically at a Starbucks) with our volunteer corps and buy them coffee. While they sipped their coffee, we would hand out flyers and go over talking points. This included who I was, why I was running, how they could encourage voters to go to my website or Facebook page, and, of course, encourage them to vote for me. I would end with some sort of motivating message and thank them all and then we would all go to our assigned routes.

At first, this was a small group of our best friends. Over time, the number would ebb and flow some, but there were typically about ten to twelve people, including Tricia and me. Modern technology made our outings fairly efficient. My campaign purchased software that had a downloadable app that generated routes for us to take. The software pulls information from voting records and selects only homes with people who have voted in at least four of the last five Republican primaries. From there, the software would organize the homes of these voters into a list, then plot the most efficient route. It's just like every other mapping software, but it also includes the names of the voters and their addresses. All in all, it was very cool and easy to use.

From our meeting place, we'd drive to the first address and then start walking and knocking. After each house, we entered information such as "will vote for Jim," "undecided," "voting for _____," and any other additional notes. At the end of each day, we exported a report from the app that compiled all the results and gave us instant feedback. Again, it was very cool.

Tricia always went with me on these outings, which made them more fun and made the time pass quickly. I always dreaded these days until we got started, but I was always exhilarated after they were over. My natural introversion would subside, and I would get in the spirit of talking to strangers about myself and whatever was on their minds. For Tricia, it was much more natural. She could get a brick wall to engage in a conversation and almost always got smiles in return from the people we spoke with. This was definitely her sweet spot. In fact, more than once, someone commented that she should be running instead of me!

A typical day started at 10:00 a.m. and would go to about 5:00 p.m. This was set because it was not too early to be a nuisance nor too close to dinner, I was told. Sunny and warm days were slower because people were out of the house. When our outings coincided with Ohio State football games, everything seemed to slow down.

At about one in four houses someone would open the door for us. The other three were a combination of nobody home or, somewhat common, was that they were home (TV on or heard voices) but wouldn't answer the door. We even got our share of drapes closing as we walked up the driveway, much like we experienced when we had to collect signatures to even start the campaign.

The doors that did open surprised us with the widest variety of people you can imagine. They included all ages, races, and species (such as the dog that could open the door on his own). Some folks would invite us in for coffee and cookies, and we'd be there an hour. Others would crack the door and take the flyer and then close the door just as quickly. Tricia ran into old friends. I ran into guys who used to work for me. We met a priest, collar and all, who walked us out and down his driveway and then held our hands and prayed for me.

We rang one door and a woman answered. She wasn't the one listed on the app but assured us she owned the home, as they recently moved in. Often, this might be a waste of time since we wouldn't know if they were a 4 or 5 but this lady proudly announced she was a Republican and invited us in. There, we met her husband and two grown sons and watched Ohio State football for fifteen minutes. While I talked football, Tricia learned all four were registered Republicans and planned to vote in the primary as usual. She also said, loudly so the men could hear, that all four would vote for me. The best door knock in our history. A four-for-one!

We encountered "No Trespassing" and "No Solicitation" signs, which we honored. Once, we came upon a "Beware of the Dog" sign after we were halfway up the driveway. As we slowly retreated, a 120-pound bullmastiff came around the back corner of the house and had his eye on us for lunch, barking madly. We reached the sidewalk just as his chain became taut and stopped his progress. We agreed to pass on this house, but then a man who appeared to be about twenty-five years old came around from the back to inspect what was going on. He was as nice as can be once he heard I was Republican and running for Congress. We spent twenty minutes talking and petting his now friendly dog.

One of our funnier meetings was at a house where no one answered the door after we rang the bell and knocked on the door. We were walking away when the garage door opened. A young couple stepped out and we introduced ourselves. They were friendly but not overly so at first. I noticed their garage was full of camping gear and also had three generators and about eight cans of gas on some shelves. As I talked to the young man, he asked more about my business and what I did for a living. He seemed intrigued. Then, he asked me, "With all those trucks and equipment you have, what do you do if the power goes out?"

I explained that we had large generators, the size of tractor trailers, and they could power our plants. His eyes opened wider.

He followed up with, "So, you're set if anything goes haywire around here, with the power plants and all, huh?"

I nodded.

"So, how much diesel you got on hand for those things?" he asked.

I wasn't sure where this was going but roughly added up our inventory and told him we usually had about 75,000 gallons of fuel at any one time.

"Wow! That's awesome! You are set, aren't you. I'll vote for you if you promise to share a little fuel if something bad happens. You know, something like nuclear." And there it was. I laughed and he spent the rest of the time talking about the world coming to an end.

One of Tricia's favorite memories was on an especially cold Saturday morning. We had met our team at Starbucks and loaded up on coffee before we hit the trail. It was sunny and clear, but the temperature was in the midtwenties when we started. Although bundled up with her warmest clothes and winter jacket, my wife is no fan of cold weather and was shivering by the time we rang our second doorbell. After about forty-five minutes, she said her feet were going numb. I noticed she had on some very nice looking leather boots, which she was very proud of, but they were not the warmest footwear. Her thin socks didn't help either.

I told her to stay in the car, but she wouldn't hear of it. She was going to tough it out. The next doorbell we rang was answered by a nice lady who smiled as soon as she opened the door. We introduced ourselves, and before I could say anything else, she was demanding we come in and warm up. As would often happen, I wound up talking to her husband for a bit while Tricia chatted with her. I could hear bits of their conversation, and it was mostly about the cold and her boots, with lots of laughter in between. By the time we were ready to leave, our hostess disappeared for a minute and returned with a pair of thick, fuzzy winter socks. She gave them to Tricia and wouldn't take "no thanks" for anything.

Tricia was exceedingly happy with her new socks on as we laughed about the whole visit while sitting in our warm car. It was another example of unexpected kindness we came to cherish as we made our way around to the homes of strangers we hoped to convert to supporters.

Our other direct outreach effort was a call center based in my office. My campaign took over a conference room and arranged desks with phones on each. We put up dividers between the desks. Baylor put together scripts and lists of people to be called. The information was culled from the same database as the door knocks so the calls were placed to 4s and 5s only.

To staff the call center, we used some of the same volunteers but about half of the callers were my employees. It was still voluntary, but my managers were very supportive in general. Maybe they wanted the boss to leave town and go to Washington, or maybe they thought I might be a good congressman. Either way, it was nice to have their support and efforts. Two of my managers, Lou and Gary, were especially supportive. The call center would start at about 5:30 p.m. (I did still have a business to run) and would continue for two to three hours. Lou and Gary were there many nights after working ten to twelve hours in the business.

I could tell they were great at this. They knew me, and they were passionate on their calls. Even as I would head out the door to go to a candidate forum, I could hear them in the conference room, and their energy was motivating for me. One morning, I came in and Gary came right over and wanted to tell me about the prior night. He was already giggling about it, and he told me the story of one of Lou's calls he overheard. Lou was being quizzed on who

I was. Then, at one point, the caller said, "You're just paid to say all that. How well do you even know Spurlino?" Lou responded "Hell, yes I know him." The guy pushed a little harder, "Really? So, how long have you known him?" Lou told the guy he'd known me for thirty-five years, worked for me for thirty-five years, and that I was the most honest and smartest guy he knew and on and on. Gary said, "Lou finishes the conversation, hangs up, looks at me, and we both just bust out laughing. Then, Lou said the guy got really nice at the end and said he'd vote for you."

This went on for weeks, and it was always interesting to hear the stories and see the tallies of what was said about voting for me. In a lot of ways, it mirrored the door knocks, although people seemed more likely to speak openly about what was on their minds over the phone.

It's hard to say enough nice things about all my volunteers. In a lot of ways, it meant more to me than people writing a check for a donation. They spent their free evenings and weekends to ask strangers to vote for me. That's a *huge* donation. My experiences finding volunteers were a lot like reaching out for the donations I received. There were some people I thought for sure would help, but they didn't. And there were others who I didn't expect to help— some of whom I'd never met—who stepped up and worked hard on my behalf. That included a number of college students from Miami University, one couple that saw me on Facebook and reached out, and one man who saw me in Starbucks with a stack of flyers and struck up a conversation that led to volunteering. It was inspiring that people took some of their precious time off to spend on my campaign. They could have been doing anything: spending time with friends and family, playing games, watching TV, or even just taking a nap, but they chose to spend that time volunteering to get me elected. And I'd never met them before.

I can't end this chapter without a shout out to my daughter, Olivia. She was a junior in high school at the time and was like a lot of high school students in that she was not particularly interested in politics. She was, however, interested in helping any way she could. She'd often find a friend to go with her and do door knocks on the weekends. Then she decided to do a bake sale to raise money. She obviously had heard me and her mom talk about raising money and wanted to help. She spent a whole weekend baking cookies and brownies, then took them to her brother's office, where a couple hundred people work. She walked up and down many halls and into many offices and told them she was selling her baked goods to raise money for my campaign. I think she raised a little less than $200. She spent a lot of time and effort to help me out. It obviously meant much more than the money to me. Thanks, sweetheart!

CHAPTER 16

Endorsements (or Lack Thereof)

AS THE CAMPAIGN MOVED FORWARD, the two opponents who were already elected officials started to roll out more and more endorsements. It was almost as if a secondary race had begun. Every week or so, one of them was announcing additional endorsements. It was no surprise that the career politicians were all supporting each other, but it did make Mark ask me the obvious question: "Can you get any endorsements? Maybe your state senator or representative or other district eight officials?" The answer was easy at the time: "I doubt it."

These other guys had long lists of endorsements, but I wondered what they really meant. Most of the endorsers were existing office-holders, but the lists also included things like, "150 Butler County Local Elected Officials," or "Group of Clark County Leaders." I asked Mark, "What the hell does a list like that even mean?" And, more importantly, "Who cares?" He agreed, and my questions seemed to start the gears moving in his head. He repeated what I said: "What *does* that even mean?" It was then that Mark hatched his idea for our last video, to be released online, or even on TV if we had enough money.

Mark's idea was to shoot a commercial in the maintenance facility of my business. This was meant to be a homespun, local shot of me at work. I would make fun of the career politicians and their endorsements and then even brag about my lack of endorsements. This would then lead me to emphasizing my independence from outside money and how I wouldn't be influenced. It made sense and certainly was a good case of making lemonade from our lemons of endorsements.

A week later, Mark had the script and we set up a time to shoot it. The message was short and to the point: "I don't have endorsements and don't want them. I won't be influenced by outsiders." Mark even arranged for photos of the endorsed candidates to pop up on the screen as I used my thumb to point at them over my shoulder. I have to admit, it came out pretty good and was aligned with the theme we had been using since the beginning. If we had a political lane created as an outsider, this was doubling down on it and making sure it was emphasized.

It never made it to TV but got decent play on social media. Overall, the response was positive, which seemed to verify that this was a good approach and one to continue. I think Mark was initially looking for the traditional endorsement track to compete, but this was a good counterpoint. It made me wonder whether endorsements should make a difference. I had rarely paid attention to endorsements in the past, as I assumed they were for political expediency or political party loyalty and not driven by true support for a candidate. When I saw the generally positive reaction to my ad, I thought that many others must feel the same way. But there would be one last decision to make on that front.

Baylor called me one morning and told me Donald Trump was coming to the Dayton area and would be holding a rally near the airport. We talked about whether to go or to release a statement of any kind regarding Trump. Throughout the campaign, I remained steadfast in my refusal to comment on the presidential primary race. It was for two reasons: I didn't want to box myself in with one candidate and risk alienating voters, and I also wasn't sure whom I preferred. At the time, Trump was gaining momentum but it was far from clear he would be the Republican candidate. Also, I wasn't thrilled with his candidacy and thought of him as more of a TV personality or something else. I wasn't even sure what that "something else" was.

Baylor had previously worked for Americans for Prosperity (AFP) in their Ohio office. During his time there, his boss's boss had been Corey Lewandowski, who was now Trump's campaign manager. He managed to contact Lewandowski, and over the course of the week they had a couple of conversations. Baylor was checking to see if there was any way I could appear at the Trump rally and get some publicity from it. Baylor's idea was that I could appear on stage with Trump, or introduce him, or have him recognize me during his remarks, or possibly even endorse me.

I was unsure whether this made sense for me or if I would be comfortable if any of it came to fruition. But it was clear from the size of crowds at Trump's events that this rally would generate a lot of publicity, and the location was in the heart of the district. I let Baylor explore all the options this might present before having to wrestle with it.

By the end of the week before Trump's visit, Baylor got final word that Trump would not be making any endorsements and would not be sharing the stage or inviting anyone up. However, he was told that Trump would welcome *my* endorsement of him. Baylor asked what I thought of endorsing Trump. Before I could answer, he laid out the positives for such a move. I admit that he made a compelling case for getting press out of it, but I had my reservations. In the end, just as I had done with this question with the *Cincinnati Enquirer* during our meeting with them, I decided I was not comfortable declaring support for any presidential candidate. My logic was not to alienate any potential voter, but I also was just plain uncomfortable endorsing Trump. We passed on this "opportunity."

CHAPTER 17

Never a Dull Moment

DURING MY CAMPAIGN, I NEVER ceased to be amazed by the frequency of oddball developments that unfolded. In this chapter, I recount several of them.

Shortly after the Trump rally, we received a call that seemed like a much better opportunity. A *Wall Street Journal* reporter had contacted Baylor to see if I was available for an interview. He was doing a story on the race to replace John Boehner and wanted to talk to the handful of candidates who appeared to be serious contenders. I loved the idea of talking to a reporter from such a highly respected national newspaper, and I jumped at the chance.

Baylor said the reporter had time the following day at 2:00 p.m. He would come to my office or meet somewhere in the south part of the district. I checked my calendar and saw an immovable appointment at that time. I had a meeting with my company's largest customer about a project that was potentially one of the largest we would have ever been involved in. I knew I could ask to reschedule it, but my strong instinct was to keep the appointment. They had several members of their top management team scheduled for this meeting, and it would be bad business practice to ask to reschedule and inconvenience them, especially in light of bidding deadlines for this project in the near future. I told Baylor to ask the reporter for an alternate time.

We tentatively rescheduled the *WSJ* meeting for the following day. Surely, the nation's leading business-focused newspaper would want to feature a businessman over career politicians. The next day, as I finished my business meeting, Baylor called with news about the *WSJ* meeting. The reporter had to cancel because he was told to immediately fly to Iowa and then New Hampshire to cover the primaries there. He said he would be back but wasn't sure when and would reschedule when he knew more. I was disappointed but hopeful that it would be sooner rather than later.

I met him a few weeks later, but not for an interview. The Associated Builders and Contractors (ABC) association had their annual dinner meeting planned, and I was asked if I wanted to attend and sit at the host table. The host table usually consisted of the association president and current chairman, the hired host for the evening, and the keynote speaker. Most would also have their wives there too. This year, ABC was going big. They had hired a well-known local radio talk show personality to host it. He was very popular, and I had just been a guest on his show.

My interview with him was generally a good experience and my first time on one of those fast-paced talk radio shows. He had a reputation as a tough interviewer, but I did not get any tough questions. The only issue I had with him or the interview was at the end. The interview had gone well. I said all the right things, he was agreeing on my positions, and it was like a conversation between two like-minded people. Then, as we finished up the interview and he thanked me for coming on, he said, "And thank you for your service to our country in the military." It was a quick-paced interview with no preparation between us of any sort and now it showed. I hadn't been in the military. Before he could go on to commercial, I quickly corrected him with, "I fully support our military and appreciate their service, but I was not in the military."

He didn't hesitate but looked a little shocked and said something acknowledging that and then went to commercial break. I just looked at him. He picked up a few pages of paper he had been referring to and said, "Well, this is off your website. You ought to take a look at it and get it corrected. It's right here." He handed me the papers, and I was escorted out of the booth as he conversed with his producer through his headphones. I looked at the pages while outside in the hallway. They were from my website, but they did not say anything about my having served in the military. There was just a paragraph in which I expressed my support for the military. Another outstanding example of journalism that helped clarify for his audience that I was not in the military.

Along with this radio personality who was to be host for the ABC event, the real draw and main feature was keynote speaker, Karl Rove. In his days since leaving the George W. Bush administration, Rove had written a book, *The Triumph of William McKinley*, which had recently been released. He'd be on hand at a VIP reception before the main event, signing books and meeting people. Baylor also told me the *WSJ* reporter would be in attendance and that he would make sure to introduce us. It sounded like a great night, although I had a candidate forum to attend afterward as well, so it was going to be a busy one as well.

Tricia and I arrived at the hotel where the event was held that evening, and we were directed to a conference room where the VIP reception was being held. We entered the door to the room and saw Karl signing books and taking photos with people. There was a line to see him, and we immediately stepped to the end of it. About fifteen minutes later, we were standing there talking to Karl. He was very affable, and the three of us chatted like old friends. It really was an unexpected surprise how easy he was to talk with and how we effortlessly carried on. Sensing that the line was getting long, someone motioned that we should move along. I started to leave, without a signature or photo, when Tricia said she needed a photo with Karl and I, and he immediately agreed.

As I turned and took a few steps for the photo, I noticed a table with his books stacked on it; next to it was a life-size cardboard cutout of George W. Bush. It was standing there next to the table and he looked great. Without thinking, I asked, "Can we have the photo taken with George? He wouldn't mind, would he?" Karl didn't hesitate and responded, "Yeah, let's go stand next to the president." Karl and I walked over to President George W. Bush, stood on either side of him, and smiled as Tricia took a few photos. I smiled broadly and shook Karl's hand and thanked him. Tricia and I wandered off into the crowd, laughing at how fun that all was. As I looked back over the next hour, I noticed we started something. Now, all the photos with Karl included President Bush.

We mingled a bit and chatted with others in the VIP room until Baylor found us and brought us over to the *WSJ* reporter. He had indeed showed up and was sipping a beer. After introductions, Baylor left us and Tricia followed to give us time to talk. The reporter apologized for missing our meeting and said we would do it soon, although not on this trip, as he was leaving in the morning. He also assured me our conversation that night was off-the-record. I believed him, although I was still a little guarded given my experience with the media and reporters.

We didn't talk issues much but just chatted generally about what it was like to cover politics for the *WSJ* and then what is was like to campaign. It felt like a social conversation and not at all on the record. I still wasn't going to say anything substantive but tried to be engaging enough that he would call back for an interview. While we stood there, he said he noticed my photo-op with Rove and Bush and humorously questioned whether that was a good thing for my campaign or not. Somehow, that led to a semiacademic conversation about George W. Bush's current reputation and future legacy as a president. I took the president's side and said his reputation was coming back and thought he would be seen very favorably in the future. The reporter was more cynical. It was an interesting conversation, one that you might have with a friend, and not too serious.

After my chat with the reporter, someone announced the main event was beginning and we should all adjourn to the ballroom. I found Tricia and we made our way to our table. John, the president of ABC, came across the room to say hello and walked us to our table at the front of the room. Sitting at the head table was an honor, and it felt special to be there. We introduced ourselves to those already seated, which was half full, and sat down. I looked at the empty seat next to me and the name tag in front of it said "Karl Rove." John was really treating us right.

Others finally joined the table. Karl sat down and I reintroduced myself and Tricia to be polite. Karl waved off the introduction as if we'd known each other for way longer than the fifteen minutes we chatted for earlier. The event began with John welcoming the crowd of about 500 or so, letting everyone know that dinner was on its way, and that the program would start afterward. It seemed that everyone at the table began conversations at once, and luckily I got another fifteen minutes with Karl before the table started asking him questions. He obliged with story after story and then became the entertainer for all of us. I looked at my watch halfway through the salad and realized that I needed to leave in about fifteen minutes to go to the candidate forum.

I was anxious to resume my one-on-one with Karl but did not get the chance until it was time to leave. I leaned over a bit and told him I had a campaign event to go to and needed to leave. I apologized that I couldn't stay and hear his remarks. He was very gracious and encouraging and said, "Oh don't worry about it. Get out of here. Go. The campaign is much more important." I thanked him again and he added, "Good luck. I know you'll be great." We said our goodbyes to the rest of the table and made our way out of the room. I told Tricia that Karl's best wishes made my night. I was feeling awesome.

We drove about thirty minutes to the candidate forum. It was being held at a local technical college building. Many of the candidates were there, but the crowd was smaller than most of the forums I had attended, probably around fifty people. Davidson was noticeably absent. He was attending fewer and fewer events. Apparently when you have a lot of money, you don't have to or want to go to these things. It reminded me of the classic sports analogy of running the clock out with a lead. There's no use risking a mistake.

We would find out later that Davidson was at an event of his own. He was down the road at a small hotel on Interstate 75, being endorsed by Ohio Congressman Jim Jordan. It appeared that a dozen or so supporters and members of the press were there, but that was it. It certainly was no surprise for any of us in the race.

It was becoming rather well known that Jordan had handpicked Davidson long ago to run for Boehner's seat. Jordan and Boehner had never gotten along, as Jordan's Tea Party thinking and his Freedom Caucus had gotten under Boehner's skin. They thwarted much of Boehner's agenda as if they were Democrats. Boehner would fume about them publicly and was said to be nuclear about them in private. Positioning a Jordan loyalist to win the Republican primary, which all but guaranteed victory in the general election, was a needle in Boehner's eye as he left office.

The event lasted a little under two hours and was unremarkable. It followed the same format and had the same questions. My energy was still up, and I was trying to enjoy the time, but it was like watching the same movie over and over. I knew how it would go, and I knew how it would end. However, tonight, the end had a funny twist. At this particular forum, two candidates showed up who were rarely at other events. One was Ed Meer. Meer is a seemingly nice guy who liked to talk to me when he *did* show up at events. He almost came off as a fan of mine, and I always took a few minutes to chat with him. During the forum, he spoke of his job as a factory worker. This usually raised some eyebrows, as that was certainly unique among us candidates. He had some typical responses and some unusual ones too. His best answer included relating the time he was homeless, living in a van. He didn't really have a point or perspective he gained from that time. It just seemed he wanted folks to know about it. One person in the audience could not resist saying "down by the river" after he said he lived in a van. It was cheap joke—referring to a *Saturday Night Live* skit that featured Chris Farley. The quip made a few people chuckle sitting near him. I just glared at them. Not funny and not the time.

The highlight of the night came at the very end. Another candidate who rarely showed up, but who was there that night, was John Robbins. This venue was close to where he lived. Robbins was seventy-seven years old and a former steel plant worker and county health department worker. He looked his age, with a medium-length, long gray beard. John was fairly plain spoken and used measured words—this is about what you'd expect from someone who spent most of his career in a steel plant. His opening comments were basic and devoid of any emotion. His answers were short and to the point. I noticed he never used the full amount of his allotted time either.

On the last question of the night, we were given a chance to make closing remarks. We could use up to two minutes to respond. Most of us who were forum regulars would use all of time or go just over, knowing we had a little leeway before getting cut off. On Robbins's turn, the moderator said, "Mr. Robbins, you have an additional two minutes to address the audience." Robbins was quiet. None of were sure he had heard the moderator, since he looked puzzled. The moderator noticed and said, "Mr. Robbins, is there anything else you want to say to the audience?" Robbins heard him for sure this time and paused. Then, he said, "No, I think I've said all I want to."

I would venture that no candidate, in any political race ever, has ever said that. The audience laughed and a few clapped. It was a great ending. He had at least won over some of the crowd for his honesty. I know I appreciated his answer and wished more politicians and candidates were like that. Tricia and I drove home reminiscing about the night and remarking how hard it is to make up stuff that rivals real life.

CHAPTER 18

The Seamy Side of Politics

MARK CALLED ME AND LEFT a message. He said he needed to talk and it was urgent. It was 2:00 p.m. on a Wednesday, and I was juggling business and campaign fundraising phone calls. The latter always seemed more like work than the former. I was realizing how much I liked running my company, which was no longer a daily grind but a welcome respite from the "work" of asking for campaign contributions.

I called Mark back to see what was so urgent. Per usual, he was calm and to the point, but this time there was something different in his voice. It wasn't his tone or inflection, but I could tell something was going on. I asked what was up, and he told me he had heard from another campaign. At this point on the call, his voice definitely betrayed his normal calm. He said he didn't want to talk about it on the phone; he needed to meet with me in person to discuss it. He also said we had to meet today. I told him I had a campaign engagement that would last until about 8:00 p.m. but could meet after that. We agreed on a restaurant in Springfield, about halfway between us, at 9:00 p.m. I tried one last time: "Want to give me a hint what we are going to talk about?" He replied that he'd rather do in it person; I begrudgingly agreed.

The rest of the day went fast, but I couldn't help but wonder what we were going to talk about. I also wondered why he was being so "cloak-and-dagger" about this. I was used to running a business and being upfront, to the point, and honest. Now I was having to deal with secrets and late-night meetings.

Finally, I finished up my day with business and campaign duties and was on the way to Springfield. I called my wife and told her of the conversation with Mark. She had the same response: "Why didn't he just tell you?"

"Who knows?" was all I could think of to say. The drive was about an hour, and all kinds of things ran through my head. Mark had done opposition research on me and came up with virtually nothing. I couldn't think of any bad news, so naturally I thought it might be good news. Maybe someone else was dropping out and wanted to support me. Maybe there was a deal to be made of some sort with another campaign.

I pulled up to one of those chain restaurants that was open late. I was a bit nervous and was hoping for a cocktail to relax until I realized it was more of a diner and alcohol wasn't available. I walked into the place and saw Mark way over in a corner by himself. He had his laptop out and was typing away. No one else was anywhere near the table. Quite the clandestine setting.

I walked up and said hi. We exchanged pleasantries and quickly got caught up on what I had been doing the past few days. Mark was a little solemn and then turned serious. I was still anticipating good news. He told me he had walked into his office that day and found a large envelope that had been slipped under the door. No markings, no name, and no address—just a blank manila envelope. He opened it and found several pages of paper with a printout of sorts. Some had more print than others. He said he didn't know who delivered it or where it came from.

Mark slid the envelope across the table. I opened it and looked over the papers. It dawned on me that the information could be damaging to me and the campaign. There was no smoking gun and certainly some plausible explanation, but the information could be damaging if spun the right (or wrong) way. Mark asked if I was aware of the information and if it was true. I stressed that it may be accurate but wasn't the whole story. I was still processing the whole thing and trying to figure out how this all got assembled and what someone—a competitor—might say about it.

Always the lawyer, Mark suggested we sleep on it and talk in the morning. He also said he would keep the papers. That way, I could say I didn't have them (or maybe never saw them?) and could not comment on them. I drove home while my mind raced. *What does this all mean? What is our competition going to do with it? What am I going to say to Tricia?*

I got home and told Tricia everything. I told her what I knew about the papers, and what I knew about what they suggested. She was completely understanding and very supportive immediately. No judgement, just unconditional support. She asked what I was going to do and what she could do to help. She gave me such an unbelievable show of support. She is such a great wife, partner, and friend.

The next day, Mark and I talked strategy on how to handle the envelope situation. There were options such as wait and deny, wait and explain, and—Mark's favorite—get out in front of it. Again, the typical lawyer, he said we would want to be the first to address it. I wasn't so sure. I felt it was embarrassing, and my gut was telling me to wait and see if it came out and then explain. There was no smoking gun, no photos, no police report, no real evidence of wrongdoing. Further, our response and explanation about it made sense to me, and I thought it was fine. Mark was fairly adamant that we should strike first but left to me to decide.

In the end, I decided to follow Mark's advice. I trusted that he was experienced in running successful campaigns and that I should follow his strategy. It didn't feel right, but it was what we did. Mark's strategy entailed filming a commercial that talked about dirty politics and highlight the envelope slipped under his door. The tweak was that we wouldn't divulge what was in the envelope, just that we received it and that we wouldn't back down. I still didn't like this, but Mark did. I guess it was his way of meeting me halfway.

A week or so later, we filmed the commercial. It was me sitting at a table with my wife, talking about the dirty politics of envelopes, and while we were at it, complaining about another campaign that was stalking my sixteen-year-old daughter on social media. That part was absolutely true and had pissed me off beyond anything else that had happened up until that point. The campaign of one of the other candidate's had been trying to "friend" our daughter on social media platforms. It was repeated and obvious. When we confronted them, they initially denied it. But then they went on to say that everyone does it so it was okay. Neither was true. It was just their despicable way of trying to get information about me and my family.

The commercial ran and we got press. "Good," said Mark. *Not sure* is what I thought. It seemed incomplete. We didn't mention what was in the envelope or any details. Just that other candidates "must fear me" and will stop at nothing. The lack of details got attention. It even got an article by the *Daily Kos* who named me "Crazy/Stupid Republican of the Day," mostly for not attacking back. Not the press I expected and, of course, I was told to ignore it. I tried, but who likes being called crazy and stupid, especially if you are trying to be the intelligent businessman running for Congress?

There was also the noticeable murmuring out on the campaign trail. Many tried to figure what was in the envelope, and others tried to figure out who sent it. The only good news was that our response was over and whatever else would happen was out of our hands. We would just deal with it, and there didn't seem to be much interest for the next few weeks.

Just as this episode appeared to be dying down, a reporter for the *Dayton Daily News,* Lynn Hulsey, called Baylor on Sunday, February 14. She had been investigating me and found that I was in arrears on child support almost fifteen years earlier but also as recently as last July. She told Baylor she had found this information in the county records and was going to publish a story. Her question was: "Any comment?" Alarm bells went off and a flurry of calls between Baylor, Mark, and me began.

I explained to both Mark and Baylor what I recalled had happened, although my memory from fifteen years before was not perfect. In essence, here are the facts that I recalled:

- My first wife and I divorced in late 1999. We had two daughters, and I was ordered to pay $3,180 per month in child support and $4,000 per month in spousal support for a total of $7,180 per month. She also received a house without a mortgage, her car, and over $200,000, among other things.
- I started my company in April 2000 and was, for a short period of time, unable to pay spousal and child support. I told her this would happen for a brief time and knew she had the house and car without payments and plenty of cash to live on.
- This continued for about three months, after which I promptly paid the balance in full with a check made out directly to her.
- The more recent arrearage was due to the slowness of the county to remove the child support order after both daughters had turned eighteen and graduated from high school, thereby removing the obligation.

Three other interesting facts:

- My oldest daughter came to live with me when she was fifteen years old. She continued to live with me until she turned eighteen and graduated. During these three years, I continued to pay child support to my ex-wife for this daughter.
- After the youngest daughter turned eighteen and graduated, I continued to pay child support for some time while waiting for the county to issue a ruling to terminate the obligation. They were slow and I stopped the payments and because of this—the agreement was labeled in arrearage.
- When the matter was settled once and for all, the county sent me a check to refund overpaid child support.

Mark and Baylor agreed that this all made sense, but we had to figure out how to prove all this to the reporter before she got it published. She was threatening to publish right away.

Throughout the years, as I paid child support there had been several times when the county claimed I was past due. They sent letters to me and my employer (my company) and made demands and threats. Each time, I would try to resolve this myself, which included several visits to the county offices and meeting with their administrative people. Each time, they would show me some printout that did not match with our canceled checks or the court order or both. And each time they would look at my information and tell me I was wrong and a deadbeat dad. Finally, I hired an attorney, Christine Haaker from Thompson Hine, to resolve this frustrating situation. Christine was great, persevered, and finally got their records straightened out. Unfortunately, it took her time (and my money) to get this done, as they would not listen to me.

My first thought now was to call Christine and get her on the case. I felt like no matter what we said to this reporter, our statements would just get printed as a denial and she would not stop the story. I called Christine's office on that same day to leave a message. It rang a few times, then an amazing thing happened. Christine answered. She was in the office catching up on some work. She listened to my story and its urgency and agreed to meet immediately. I was in my car in minutes and on my way to her office.

We sat and discussed the details and storyline the reporter was threatening. She had some files but not anything for the last several years since there had been no more mistakes or issues. She agreed to work on it right away but also had a time conflict. She was leaving the next day for depositions out of town and would be gone for several days and generally unavailable. In any case, she said she would do the best she could and reach out to the reporter ASAP.

Christine talked to this reporter and confirmed what Baylor and Mark suspected. The reporter wasn't interested in facts or the whole story; she just wanted a comment for her story. Christine sent a few emails that day and the next, succinctly quoting Ohio law and attaching numerous documents showing I was not in arrears. She also stated the fact that I continued to pay child support for a daughter that lived with me rather than seek an end to that arrangement. Finally, she made it clear that she had all the records, thousands of pages from the county, that she would share with the reporter along with other court records and check stubs as soon as her prior commitment with depositions ended. She just needed forty-eight hours and would then clear her schedule and meet or talk.

More emails went back and forth between Christine and the reporter. Christine stated clearly that she was in depositions and could speak to her on Wednesday. The reporter then added demands for information about the cyberstalking of our daughter and other matters. Finally, this reporter said she had to speak to someone before Wednesday.

Our only other strategy was to get my ex-wife to talk to the reporter or send a signed statement. I talked to her about this, and she seemed reluctant but then agreed. We asked her to state the simple truth: I was briefly in arrears, then I paid it all back in full. Mark sent her a statement to sign that we could send to the reporter. We waited to receive it back as promised, thinking it would help our case or, even better, stop the story from going to print. She ended up sending an email saying the statement is true and that I am great father, but she didn't want to get involved.

Whatever happened to having a spine and standing up for what's right? At that point, I wished I hadn't sent that extra child support for three years while my daughter was living with me.

After a whole two days, one being Sunday, without a meaningful conversation with Christine or review of any of the mountain of information we had, the *Dayton Daily News* printed on its front page a picture of me and the headline "Records: 8th district candidate was past due on child support payments." They offered no explanation for the rush to publish.

Was the headline true that the records showed I had been past due on child support? Yes. They get credit for that being accurate. That is it though. They wouldn't wait to talk with my attorney who had all the records, knowledge, and expertise to walk the reporter through the facts. Their interest in getting to press with the attention-getting headline apparently trumped everything else.

The whole episode made me angry. It was one thing to have the article impact the campaign, but it was way worse being called a deadbeat dad in the wake of the story. That is abhorrent. It ate at my soul and continues to bother me today.

The week after the *Dayton Daily News* article published its child support article, there was a candidate forum in Clark County. Clark is a somewhat rural county with a population of 135,000, although its largest city, Springfield, has 60,000. It would be a mix of rural and small city folks but certainly still conservative.

This forum was held at a junior high school, and the students were encouraged to attend. It was somewhat encouraging to become involved with something that a teacher spearheaded. In fact, during the Q&A portion of the event, the students were the ones asking the questions, and the teacher made it clear that the students came up with their own questions. They went as far as assigning a student to ask a particular candidate a question, so the questions were all unique and only that candidate answered the question.

To begin the forum, we went through the normal opening statements, and then, using a predetermined order, the teacher called a candidate to the podium to get their question directly from the student who wrote it. It looked like the students were seventh and eighth graders, and the first few questions were good, although they were somewhat standard fare. The crowd seemed to be into this new and unusual format, and the candidates were enjoying it as well.

When my name was called, I walked to the front of the stage. I was handed a microphone and stood front and center. A girl's name was called, and she walked to a microphone stand in the audience area and started her question for me. I walked over a few feet from she was standing, still on the stage. Her voice was clear, and she did not seem nervous. She then stated that there had been an article in the *Dayton Daily News* last week about my being late on child support and asked if I'd like to explain this or address it. The crowd let out a mix of groans, oohs, and ahs. Many of the adults in the audience were visibly uncomfortable with the question, and it was obvious many thought it was inappropriate. No one, including me, expected this question from a student.

The one fortunate thing about the timing of this question was that I was very prepared to talk about this issue. I had been dealing with the article and the impact of terrible reporting over the previous week and a half. As soon as she was done and the crowd reacted, I interjected immediately and said to the audience, "No, no, no. That's okay. That's alright." The crowd quieted down. I looked right at my questioner and said, "I'm glad you asked that question because I do want to talk about this and explain what the paper didn't say and how that reporter handled the whole thing."

I turned back to the audience as I walked back to the center of the stage and began my explanation. I took my time and went through it, hitting the salient points. I made sure everyone knew I wasn't hiding from anything and that the only wrong was from a reporter and newspaper who couldn't wait to publish a salacious hit piece on me without getting the all the facts.

I finished and felt the audience genuinely appreciated getting the whole story and was sympathetic to me. Although there were surely people there who had rushed to judgment based on the incomplete reporting, I think most were understanding that there was more to the story that the media chose not to hear before going to press.

Not all media is corrupt, but there are enough media outlets with questionable ethics that the public has started to change its opinion on what they read. "Don't believe everything you read," and "take it with a grain of salt," are phrases that have been around a long time for a reason.

My impression from the stage was reinforced after the event as Tricia and I mingled with the crowd. There was probably not another event during the campaign where I got as many people walking up to me and expressing their support or approval. The young girl who asked the question even made it over for a handshake. I smiled and said to her, "Good question. I'm glad you asked it."

CHAPTER 19

More Media Activity

MARK WAS ALWAYS LOOKING FOR ways to get media attention for my campaign. The difficulty was that there were ongoing campaigns throughout Ohio and the country; standing out was almost impossible. It was compounded by the fact that it was a presidential election year and the commentary about it dominated the airwaves and print. As President Obama's State of the Union address neared, Mark called with an idea.

"I just read that Obama plans to have illegal immigrants as guests at the State of the Union address. I want to put out a presser [press release] that denounces it and calls on the Capitol Police to arrest them. If you agree, I'll write something up and send it to you. It should generate some attention." It sounded pretty straightforward, so I said sure.

After my meeting, I checked my email on my phone and saw Mark had sent the press release draft. I opened it and saw an attachment that I assumed was his draft for this. Sitting in my car, I read through it. It was typical for Mark—attack-style and to the point. We did end up releasing the presser, and it attracted some notice. However, it was not for all the right reasons. What Mark had read was information about the *prior* year's State of the Union address where there were illegal immigrants as guests. He was reading a rehash of an old story, thinking that it was regarding the upcoming address.

Some reacted positively to our calling out the practice of bringing illegal immigrants into the capital, while others saw the error and called me out for misinformation. Not our finest hour.

As the race came down to its final thirty days, the media became more active and had Baylor fielding more requests for interviews and statements. The uproar from the child support issue had faded considerably and was not mentioned in any further media, nor did it come up at any subsequent candidate forums. As Mark and I chatted one day to brainstorm how to get more and better media coverage, he started probing me a bit on issues he felt would get notice.

At that particular time, Trump was gaining more traction among voters, which was good for a fellow outsider like me, but it also drove more of the attention to whatever he was saying. At that point, the border wall was getting a lot of mentions and seemed popular nationally as well as in the conservative heart of the congressional district. Tricia and I noticed this every weekend as we made our rounds knocking on doors and talking to people.

Although I had read enough to know that there was a need to strengthen security along the U.S.–Mexico border, I didn't see it as the main issue. The way I thought about it was that national security was an imperative focus followed by immigration. I felt strongly that national security is the primary responsibility of those in federal office. If we don't have national security, then all else is at risk. I also felt that our national security was probably better than ever, as the 9/11-driven improvements in intelligence and defense had seemed to be working. I just didn't detect that there was a serious national security issue that wasn't being addressed and certainly not from the lack of a wall along our southern border.

As for immigration, I knew our country had not adequately addressed immigration reform. However, a precursor to modernizing our immigration policies is to secure the border. I simply did not believe you could rewrite immigration policy and expect it to work if there was not a secure border. What's the point of rebuilding the town below the dam when the dam still leaks and is getting worse every day?

I also felt strongly about immigration policies because my grandfather was an immigrant. He came to America through Ellis Island from Italy when he was just nineteen years old. He worked hard, got married, and had two children. He also became an American citizen. He followed all the rules and eventually was granted this honor. I still remember hearing that when asked if he was Italian, he would always respond that he was American. He was extremely proud of that, as am I of him. My opinions on immigration are that we should respect those who follow our rules and welcome them. For those who do not follow the rules, there should be consequences—including deportation.

The trouble for me at the time was that we as a country were behind in figuring out how to deal with the immigrants who had crossed our border and had been living in the United States for years or sometimes decades. Many were law-abiding people who were gainfully employed and raising families. However, many were also not paying taxes or their "fair share." It all needed addressing in a humane, fair, and equitable way. I believed in setting a path to citizenship for some, a path to legal residence without citizenship for some, and deporting others. However, first we needed to secure the border!

It was obvious to me that there were stretches along the border that needed reinforcing and others that needed additional walls. The entire border did not need, nor was it logical to build, a wall. Portions of a wall were one piece of border security that needed to work in tandem with other strategies—including intelligence; high-tech monitoring; proper resourcing to high-risk areas, ocean and sea ports, rail border crossings, airports, etc. There was clearly much more than just a Mexican border wall problem. However, Trump was constantly talking about a wall, so the media tended to pick up a lot of related content. That was when Mark had another idea.

"If Trump and the media have made the wall such a big deal, and people want to see it built, is there any chance your company could do it? I mean, couldn't you build a wall down there? I'm really asking, could you offer to build the wall?" I was silent. I knew Mark was looking for an angle, but he didn't really understand my business. I told him that my company manufactures and delivers concrete. We are a "supplier" to companies that are contractors. And contractors build walls, not my company.

Thinking this was done, and being wrong about that, I waited for Mark to move on, but he kept on. "Okay, so you can't build the wall. Could you supply the concrete for the wall?" The theoretical answer was "yes," but I knew where he was going and knew he may not understand that it is much more complex in the real world. I replied, "Of course we can. But you know there is more to it than just being able to supply a project. There has to be a design for the wall and a scope that includes where, how long, and other details. Then, there's a prequalification and—"

Mark interrupted. "I know there is much more. I'm just asking *could* you do it. You said yes, so my next question is would you do it for free? For your country?"

I thought he had to be joking, but we continued the conversation. "Of course not," I began, sensing his objective, "but I'd probably do it for cost. No profit added. Just cover costs and overhead." I was thinking in reality to some degree; my logic was that (a) we could do it; (b) we could cover lots of overhead; and (c) we would reap a hell of a lot of publicity doing it. The biggest "of course" was that this would never happen, but Mark had the answer he wanted.

"Okay, then we put out a presser stating you'll supply concrete for the border wall. I think it just might get some attention, maybe statewide, maybe even national. I'll start working on it now and get you a draft." Within an hour, Mark forwarded a draft that I read through, made a few changes to, and sent back. He said he'd get it released ASAP. I didn't think much of it or, more accurately, I thought, *There goes Mark.* About a week and a half later, *USA Today* published an article under the headline, "Boehner seat candidate: I'll supply concrete for border wall."[14] Below the headline was a picture of Donald Trump touring the Mexican border. The article was short but a good attention-grabber and generally positive. It read:

> *If Donald Trump needs any help fulfilling his promise to build a wall along the U.S.–Mexico border, he'll find a volunteer in Ohio.*
>
> *Jim Spurlino, owner of Middletown, Ohio's, Spurlino Materials and a candidate for Ohio's 8th Congressional District, offered to send his company's "mobile concrete plants" to the border to build a barricade that prevents immigrants from coming across illegally.*
>
> *Immigration experts said Spurlino's offer is a clever publicity stunt, if not a serious policy proposal.*

> *"It's a great PR move for his company,"* Marguerite Telford,
> *a spokeswoman for the Center for Immigration Studies, which*
> *opposes legal status for those now in the U.S. illegally. "And I*
> *think it's a great PR move for him because as we have learned*
> *through Trump, talking about immigration enforcement . . .*
> *resonates with the public."*

In the middle of the electronic version of the article, there was a link with the title "Trump: When audiences get bored I use 'the wall.'" I thought to myself that that link and the article itself were proof Mark was right and his instincts got me press. The reaction was generally positive. Some people were a bit skeptical, just as a quote in the article noted (I think humorously): "You can't just appear down there on property with cement trucks." But all in all, it was press and I got noticed.

I was pleased outwardly, but inside I had mixed emotions. I knew it was publicity that was going to get me noticed and would be generally positive in the district. I also knew it would get people talking and could help in candidate forums. The "mixed" part came from the fact that I knew it was an offer that would never get taken up or taken seriously and not something I would ever say unless cajoled by Mark. I wasn't embarrassed by it, but it just wasn't me. It felt inauthentic. It was another time that Mark persuaded me to say or release something that was sensationalistic. It was not his fault by any means. I was ultimately in charge and responsible for everything that went out in my name; nonetheless, it was another episode where I was a little uneasy.

Weeks of candidate forums went by, and there were a few mentions of the *USA Today* article by voters before and after the events. For the most part, these forums continued to be dominated by rote answers to questions that most of us were knowledgeable about and used to answering. At times, there would be new questions, but they were rarely meaningful to the event. Despite this, several of us started standing out as articulate and well versed in the issues. During this time, it became obvious which candidates were serious contenders and which ones were not.

I think some of those who did not appear to be contenders were simply not taken seriously due to a lack of effort put forth throughout the campaigning period. Some candidates hardly ever appeared at forums. Others attended only the ones near their homes or in their home counties. When these part-timers did attend a forum, they often were not prepared, or not as prepared as the serious contenders, and it showed. Their answers would sound vague, or they would wander through their answers. This all tended to affect the number of mentions in newspapers or on television and gave the overall impression of who was being talked about as a potential Boehner replacement.

With a little over a month to go, Baylor received an invitation for me to attend a forum not previously announced or known. It was from the *Cincinnati Enquirer*, the largest newspaper in the area, especially in the southern half of the district. The invitation was from the editorial board; they asked me to provide written answers to a set of questions and then attend a meeting with them for further questions. The two major differences were that the forum would be closed to the public, and they were only inviting five candidates. Baylor and I were both pretty excited. Although not official, it appeared I made a first cut of sorts with this invite. The others invited were the two current politicians, Derickson and Beagle, along with Davidson, the other businessman, and White, the airline pilot.

We pored over the questions and discussed them in general. Then, Baylor drafted responses for me to review. As an aside, it may seem like I should personally answer these questions and let Baylor and Mark review. The practical side is that there were about one hundred such requests over the course of the campaign. Some are long and some are short. Some ask a lot of yes/no or for/against questions, and others allow space for one to elaborate. In any case, it was most practical for Baylor and Mark to handle drafting these responses. It freed me up to do things that required my personal presence, whether on the phone or in person. There simply wasn't time for me to do all things.

Baylor's answers to the *Enquirer*'s questions were more feisty than usual. He seemed to be finding a voice and pitch that were more pointed than early on in the campaign. The writing was crisp as usual but had a new edge. As I reread the answers, I kept getting stuck on a new word he used: "feckless." I knew the word but never used it myself in any conversation. It was one of those words that seemed sporadically written but rarely spoken. After I checked the internet to verify its definition (lacking initiative or strength of character; irresponsible), I called Baylor to discuss final draft answers and ask him about "feckless." He told me that it was one of his favorite words, and he did indeed use it in conversation. He also defended where he used it in my answers as "a perfectly accurate description of current leadership in Washington."

"Okay then," I responded, and we left it in. I figured I'd have to get used to saying "feckless" once in a while.

On the day of the forum, Baylor and I arrived at the *Enquirer*'s office and rode the elevator up to their executive floor. It was strangely empty but not a surprise. The *Enquirer* had experienced several years of cutbacks and staff layoffs. The paper's size and content had suffered noticeably. Their deterioration in quality and distribution had been a regular source of conversation in Cincinnati.

We were led into a conference room where a few staffers lingered. The other candidates were filing in, and we were all instructed to sit on one side of the conference table. Baylor and other campaign staff were told they could stand against a wall on the opposite side. Then the editorial board members strode in along with a few other folks; the other folks were introduced as members of local chambers of commerce. I didn't recognize anyone.

An older gentleman, who I assumed was the editor in chief, introduced everyone on his side of the table and explained the format. It was similar to the other forums in that there would be a question and each candidate would respond. The order would change each time. There were no formal time limits, but it was clear they were looking for brevity.

The questions were not as cookie-cutter as in other forums. Some seemed more thoughtful, such as ones about working with Democrats, but others were pure nonsense. It was the latter ones that shocked me most. I had a hard time, and probably failed, in hiding my disdain. Here are two examples of their professional journalistic efforts:

In what I can only assume was their effort to discern our commitment to racial issues, they asked each of us to respond to a question of which we preferred: Black Lives Matter (BLM) or All Lives Matter. They made it clear they wanted a simple answer of one or the other and that's it. I know my face betrayed my inner voice saying, *Are you kidding me? No discussion at all?!* I looked around the room and for the first time noticed that about half of the other side of the table was black. It felt like a relevant topic, but not allowing discussion seemed like pandering at best and a setup at worst.

It is worth noting that at the time, which was early 2016, BLM was closer to its infancy than today. It was less defined and less cohesive. It was just starting to become something more than a set of unrelated protests and banners in many parts of the country, and the Eighth Congressional District had not experienced much documented racial discord and certainly no protests. Cincinnati, however, had a long history of racial incidents, including riots as recently as 2001. There was a greater sensitivity to these issues in metropolitan Cincinnati than in the Eighth Congressional District. You could also say that no one in the district felt like they lived in Cincinnati. It was a big city with problems to the south. People in our area didn't consider Cincinnati was part of us. In any case, whether through ignorance or lack of urgency from lack of problems, the district was not up to speed on BLM. In fact, the district was proud of its historical lack of racial unrest and generally welcoming attitude.

It is also worth noting that the term "All Lives Matter" was not seen as a "term" by many at all in the district. It was more of a simple statement—U.S. Senator Tim Scott, a black Republican, had used it—and was not viewed as an affront to BLM. At the time, most from the district would have commented that "of course, all lives matter" and never would have thought making such a statement could be construed as racist. The thinking would simply be that all races and ethnicities are important and to be valued. Of course, BLM doesn't mean anything different.

I was fourth in line for answering and looked down the line as the first candidate replied, "*all* lives matter," with an emphasis on "all." The second candidate gave the same answer, with the same emphasis. So did the third candidate. I cleared my voice and started to explain that BLM is a movement that has meaning and aspirations while, "All Lives Matter" is not. I was immediately shot down and told they were looking for an answer only, not an answer plus an explanation. My mind raced, and I knew I had to answer and not argue. What a stupid and awful position to be in. I answered with even more emphasis than the others before me with "ALL lives matter," and then added quickly before they could move on, "EVERY life matters." I was pissed off at them and at myself. I should have refused to answer unless given an opportunity to speak. This was far from a topic that deserves only a check-the-box answer. The fifth answer was the same as I sat there and wondered whether the five of us looked racist or ignorant or both. The idiotic condescending looks from across the table gave me my answer. I just stared back clearly looking frustrated with the proceedings.

The second example is less shocking but reinforces the ineptitude in the room. A big issue of that time was the bridge carrying Interstates 71 and 75 across the Ohio River between Kentucky and Ohio. It had long since reached its capacity and had been causing long delays and accidents for many years. Most people in the region, on both sides of the river, knew it to be a problem and knew it needed to be fixed. It needed to be replaced, enlarged, rerouted, or some combination of them all. The question from the editorial board was: "As a congressman, what will you do to fix this problem?"

I was surprised at the question for a simple reason. We all were running for a federal office, in the federal government, to do work for our country while representing our district. The solution to the bridge problem was one that had to be worked out by Ohio and Kentucky. It was part of an interstate that may get partial funding by the U.S. government, but any solution must be agreed to by the two states and funded by the two states. Any federal dollars involved would flow through the states and be used at the discretion of those states. The holdup then was agreeing to that funding—essentially Ohio wanted a toll road and Kentucky did not. (A depressing update: there has still been no progress on this as of this book's printing, and no progress seems likely in the near future.)

My initial thought to answering this question was to start to explain the reality of the situation and how to resolve it. My frustration got the better of me, and I said, "Nothing," and paused for effect. Before I could begin the explanation part of my answer, I got disbelief and chagrin and, "What do you mean 'nothing'?" from one of the editors. I briefly explained how interstates and bridges get funded and built and that as a U.S. congressman there was nothing I could do to make Ohio and Kentucky build a new bridge. I was quickly cut off again, and they moved on to the next candidate for their answer.

The forum wound down with less nonsense but not much more substance. As it came to a close, they told us they would be writing a piece and likely give a recommendation for one candidate. Earlier in the forum, they had joked that it was like a job interview, so I circled back to that to make one last point. I suggested they talk to references. I explained they should talk to people who know each of us and have worked with each of us to get a real sense of who we are and whether we are likely to get things done in Washington. For my part, I gave them three references right then and there in front of everyone. Each was highly respected and known by most of the editorial board: a former CEO of Procter & Gamble, the city's largest employer; the CEO of a nonprofit serving primarily black at-risk families with young children (where I was chairman of board); and a prominent black minister whom I had worked with over the years. I thought that was a great exclamation point. A clear offer to check on me with people who know me and that they trusted as well. No other candidate said a word. (Later, after the election was over and I had spoken to each of my references, I was not surprised to learn none of them reported having been contacted.)

The *Enquirer* staff thanked us for our time, and we all got up and shook hands around the room. After I thanked the gentleman running the meeting, he said he wanted to ask one more question of me. "Why did you call our current leaders feckless in our questionnaire? What did you mean by this?" I looked at him and paused. Here is a guy who presumably has a decent vocabulary and command of the English language. I didn't ask the question back I wanted to: *What don't you understand about being feckless?* That would have been way too much fun. Instead, I was pleasant and gave him a vanilla answer about lacking leadership and character and being ineffective. He didn't seem to buy it, but that's how feckless people are.

About a week later, the *Enquirer* released their article. I didn't expect to get the full endorsement and I didn't. However, they were actually somewhat complimentary, although they took one semishot at me.

First, they commented on military versus legislative experience. For some reason, and it is common, they determined that the two candidates with military experience, White and Davidson, have "the best understanding of the situation in the Middle East." In their forum as well as every other forum, this was never evident. They also mentioned that I had "demonstrated leadership in attacking important regional issues at the community level" and that the two politicians, Beagle and Derickson, "have legislative experience." There was no opening mention of Davidson.

Then, they came out and essentially endorsed Derickson, although it was without using the word "endorsement." They praised his experience "in the minority party as well as the majority party" and "the ability to put politics aside to advance his legislative agenda." They praised his comments on immigration, same-sex marriage, and the U.S. Supreme Court. Regarding the supreme court and Obama's forthcoming nomination, his comment that "it would be a chance to put our country first—not ideology or gridlock" seemed to seal the deal for these editors.

In a section titled "Two strong runners-up for the 8th," they mentioned me and Davidson. They thought we "have shown promise in this race and could be strong public servants with a little seasoning." They also recommended we both "consider running for county or statehouse positions where [we] can develop [our] voices, sharpen [our] positions and show [our] ability to advance agendas." Thanks for the advice on becoming a career politician.

Their one critical comment about me was the following: "The Spurlino who met with the editorial board doesn't mesh, however, with the one who wrote that Ohio's Medicaid expansion was 'a sad decision by feckless leaders. It shackled able-bodied adults—by the hundreds of thousands—into poverty with poor quality health care.'" In this instance, they had poached a quote out of a larger text where I talked about Medicaid's poor quality of care and lack of basic services to help those in need. The actual point I was making was to improve the system to include more comprehensive services, such as mental health, maternal health, and wraparound services for children ages zero to three years old. I think they missed it because they were focused on the part with Baylor's favorite word in it: "feckless." As Forrest Gump might have said to them, "Feckless is as feckless does!"

CHAPTER 20

Social Media

SOCIAL MEDIA IS INCREDIBLY POWERFUL, and some of the pitfalls associated with this power have come into sharper focus even in the short time since my campaign ended. Nonetheless, social media is a must for political candidates. Its ability to reach large numbers of people quickly and cheaply is astounding compared with traditional media. There was never a question that I would need to be present on social media during my campaign. The only question was how.

In my business and personal life, I had never had a presence on social media. My business had a website that only let people know we existed. It also had a Facebook page with the main purpose of recruiting new employees. I never had any personal accounts. I was typical of, or even a bit behind, many my age who knew some about all these platforms but did not participate.

Mark and Baylor had ideas about all this. Of course, there was a campaign website, but they also created accounts for me on

Facebook, Instagram, Twitter, and LinkedIn. The "big four" of that time. Very quickly, all four had pictures, videos, and quotes from me. I was posting on all four almost every day. Except, it wasn't really "me" doing the posting. Baylor was at first, then we had help from one of the Miami University Young Republicans who we paid to assist the campaign. My comments on local and national news were posted regularly. Photos of me at events, video from door-knocking, and every other major and minor campaign event would get posted somewhere or everywhere.

I had only limited knowledge about what was being posted. Baylor was handling it either directly or through oversight, and I trusted him. He would tell me about these postings either just before or just after he put them up. If it was going to be significant or a quote from me, he would always run it by me for approval, but for the most part I was hands off. I couldn't even tell you what my passwords were or how to access any of them.

It all worked well, although there were several occasions when people would say to me that they saw a tweet or a video on Instagram, and I would have to nod my head and try not to expose the whole operation. It was kind of funny, but I also felt disingenuous. I would guess this was common practice back then and maybe even standard operating procedure for most politicians today.

While my social media presence was positively received, some of the comments posted were either negative or bizarre or both. Baylor would keep me informed about how things were trending. It was generally a recap of how many "likes" or "follows" and some highlights of comments. Every now and then he would share some of the funnier ones too.

He would let me know of the negative ones or if he thought we should respond, but there weren't many overall and we rarely engaged with the few that did appear. One of the funnier ones popped up on Facebook a few weeks after my video was shot. Mark had been using the video in multiple places and also used some still shots for various press releases. One viewer of the video showing me shooting my pistol wrote to say that I wasn't holding the pistol properly and did not know what I was doing.

Baylor relayed all this but said there was no need to respond. I, on the other hand, was feeling a little indignant about it and told him I was holding it the exact way I should and, in fact, had been trained by a SWAT commander during a gun safety and proficiency class the previous year. I was already plotting my response when Baylor assured me that I didn't need to respond and doing so might start a back-and-forth that we don't want to get into. "Just let it go," he said. "Anyone who knows guns and sees the video will know you're proficient and can handle a gun." He was right, but I was still unhappy. A minor gun skirmish on Facebook was not our goal.

Of the negative commenters and posters, one troll was particularly persistent. Baylor called me one morning and asked if I knew a particular person who had posted on my Facebook page. He said this troll said some pretty negative things about me during the time I was a partner in a car dealership. Apparently, she was an employee of the dealership and was fired at some point.

Her name sounded familiar, and I recalled that she worked for a short time at the dealership and our general manager had fired her. I didn't remember any particulars about the situation or having been part of the decision. In fact, I wasn't sure I had spoken to her at all more than an introduction when she started and a few passing hellos after that. She, however, seemed to have plenty to say about me.

Over the following days, she continued to post almost daily on my Facebook page in the public view section, and Baylor continued to delete her comments each time. At some point, it seemed to become a game. Baylor was waking up earlier and earlier in the day to check my Facebook page and delete her comments, which were becoming more and more derogatory. He attempted to block her, but apparently it took a while for some reason, so he continued to rise at 5:00 a.m. to scrub her comments. Finally, the block took hold and she was gone.

It was bizarre, almost to the level of cyberstalking. I'm not sure how I became her target since we barely met, and I was not involved in day-to-day management, but she must have assumed I was responsible for her eventual firing at my dealership and her unhappiness about it. It was good to be done with the distraction, and Baylor started sleeping in a little later.

I think Tricia and I knew there would be some unkind things said about me. It is just the nature of political campaigns and part of what you sign up for. I was okay with the thought of this happening and made sure that Tricia was okay with it as well, for our kids' sake too. At the start of the campaign, Mark had confirmed that we could expect attacks on me, although he did not anticipate anything too nasty. He also said that a general rule was that spouses and children are off limits and that even in the worst campaigns that remained true.

While this was the case throughout the campaign, one other candidate obviously didn't get the memo and went beyond anything I'd consider reasonable. Our daughter, Olivia, who was sixteen years old at the time, began getting friend requests online from people she didn't know. She was smart enough to decline these, but one was persistent. Tricia and I looked into it and while we were not sure, it appeared to come from the campaign of another candidate.

I talked to Mark and Baylor about this and passed on the information that Olivia had online from this person. They did indeed track it to a person on the campaign staff of a competitor. I was furious and astonished. What kind of person, a male adult no less, tries to "friend" a sixteen-year-old daughter of another candidate? Mark and Baylor huddled, and it was decided they should reach out to the campaign manager about this staffer and his activity. I reluctantly agreed; I really wanted to call the candidate myself, but I decided to follow their lead.

A day later it was confirmed it was a staffer and his campaign manager apologized and agreed to put a stop to it. They claimed ignorance as to her age at first, but then they continued and explained it was common practice to get information on a competitor and his or her family. I said it was perverted and beyond basic societal norms. We did end up doing some media coverage of this event because I was so incensed. There were the usual denials, but it never went much further and the activity stopped.

I would have fired the staffer on the spot, but the other candidate took no action. For me, it would be inexcusable. It's not very hard to lose respect for people who do these kinds of things, but apparently some live with themselves just fine. It was also another example of how social media can contribute to nefarious behavior. Before social media existed, I can't imagine a campaign hiring a private detective to follow around my sixteen-year-old daughter. But now that such contemptuous behavior was so easy, it has enabled those lacking a moral compass.

CHAPTER 21

The Campaign Heats Up

WE WERE DOWN TO THE final three weeks before election day, and the surge of outside money made me progressively less confident about my chance to win. I wasn't quitting and neither was anyone on my team. We remained optimistic and rarely spoke of the reality of the funding disparity. I continued to spend some time at my office each day, but I increasingly spent time calling and seeing people, mostly to try to raise money.

The calls and conversations between the campaigns seemed to be picking up. It was always between campaign managers and/or political consultants. The only time the candidates talked to each other was at events, and the top-tier candidates kept their comments guarded.

Mark made one call at my request. Baylor had received a message through my website from a man who claimed to have information that one of my biggest rivals had used "inside information" to acquire property from another man with dementia. There wasn't much information in the message itself, but he was offering to share this with us. He made it clear that this candidate had done something that if not illegal was at least unethical and immoral.

The two prevailing theories that supported talking to this man were: (1) do whatever it takes to win and (2) knock out a top-tier opponent and possibly reap the benefits of attracting his supporters. It had the potential to be a game changer, especially if the opponent's supporters were likely to overlap with me, which we believed to be the case.

Baylor forwarded me the email at 9:41 a.m. Mark and I chatted on the phone briefly, and I made it clear where I stood. We hung up, but I wanted to make sure I was crystal clear. I sent him and Baylor an email at 10:02 a.m. that read, "Make sure he knows we have no interest in this." Since the guy's email contained his own name, I also told Mark we should let the other candidate know. Regardless of anything else, I was not going to let myself or my team become involved in this. There had been enough envelopes.

More silliness followed later that week. The Club for Growth—Davidson's major outside money source, compliments of Congressman Jim Jordan—sent an email announcing their endorsement of Davidson. I'm not sure why they did this, as there could not have been more than one hundred people in the district who didn't know this or even cared. But the outrageous part of their email was an attack on me, Beagle, and Derickson. We were clearly the biggest challengers. Of Beagle and Derickson, it was the typical complaints derived from their voting records as elected office holders. This included voting for Medicaid expansion and tax hikes.

When the email went after me, they had only two items. The first was my $500 contribution to Senator Sherrod Brown. Okay, no big deal and I could explain this minor contribution for what it was—access to the senator to discuss early childhood issues. The second item was different. It said, "Has stated he will self-fund with $1 million of his own money." This was patently a lie. I never said that, ever, to anyone, and had no intentions of doing so.

I was a bit outraged that the Club for Growth—supposedly an upstanding, ethical, and honest organization—would print such a thing and send it out to all their members and supporters. Mark and I had a call about this, and obviously there was little to do about it before the election, but he suggested having an attorney send them a letter asking them to back up their accusation. I took little solace in this idea but told Mark to go ahead and send something to them. They should at least know their emails contained lies and try to do better while we threatened them with a lawsuit.

I tried to put the craziness of the campaign out of my mind even as these and many other irrelevant things came and went. I was determined to make the best showing possible and salvage what was left of my pride. I had been proud of my commitment to run for office, to offer intelligent and informed opinions and insights on the critical issues of the day, and to sacrifice my private life for public service. Now, I felt like it was every other day of nonsense and was growing tired of that.

One of my favorite "forums" was more of a group meeting where I was the only candidate. Baylor had been chairman of the Miami University College Republicans (MUCR) during his student days. It was not that many years ago, and he still knew a handful of the members of this group. The MUCR is a fairly large student organization and the members meet regularly to discuss public policy and ideology. They also seek out speakers for their meetings such as members of Congress, state representatives and senators, and other political operatives. They invited me to come speak to them.

Baylor and I made the trip to the campus in Oxford, Ohio, one cold February evening. We walked into an auditorium-style classroom where some students sat and others were still filing in. Baylor found the current chairman and spoke with him. I was the agenda item that evening and was happy to see a healthy turnout. When the chairman called the meeting to order, there were about forty students spread out in the seats but all closer to the front than the back. It was a purely voluntary meeting, and it was good to see an interested crowd.

I had my customary uniform on that included gray slacks, a blue button-down shirt, and a blue blazer. I almost never wore a tie because I felt it was a bit formal and wanted to appear as approachable as possible. The chairman introduced me, and I thanked them all for showing up on a cold evening when they obviously had many different options for how to spend their time, including studying. It was a small laugh line but it worked. My remarks were only about fifteen minutes and followed my stump speech mostly. I really wanted to engage them in conversation more than anything else, so I left plenty of time for Q&A.

I was very impressed with what followed. Every question was thoughtful, and most had follow-ups to their original. It soon became the conversation I was hoping for at other forums. These students were more prepared than most of the audiences I had experienced before. They probed every issue that was in the headlines and then quite a few more that weren't. They put to rest any fears I might have had that the next generation didn't care about government and politics.

The rest of the evening went quickly, and I enjoyed my time immensely. I felt a little like a professor holding class but also as if I was having a spirited conversation at home with my kids. They respected me and my opinions but would not hold back if they thought otherwise. I left wishing that more of the candidate forums were like this but mostly was proud to see that this slice of the younger generation cares a lot about our country.

One of the final candidate forums was to be held in Hamilton, Ohio, the largest city in the district. All of the candidates were invited, including Democrats and those from third parties. It was hard to tell how many candidates would show up, but I assumed it would be quite a few based on the location. Baylor, Tricia, and I arrived early as we always did and made sure we knew where the building was. As we sat in the car, we saw Davidson walking with his entourage. This was more common now, as he seemed to have more and more people accompanying him. He had a young man whose sole responsibility seemed to be driving him in the family minivan. As he walked toward my car, he stopped. I could tell he didn't know where he was going and looked lost. He then started walking again, down a side street, the exact wrong way and away from the event. I rolled down my window and yelled to him. He kept going, thinking I was just saying hello, and waved back. I said a little louder, "Warren! You're going the wrong way. The event is down the street you just passed. Third building on the right." He turned around and came back by my car, saying thanks, and then down the correct street. Baylor looked at me. I said, "Oh, what the hell. He gets lost easy." We grinned at each other and got out of the car to go inside.

The room for the event was packed solid. It was the typical mix of people ranging from college students to senior citizens and, of course, the press. The room seemed like two classrooms put together that were meant to hold about fifty students, but it seemed like twice that amount. I did a little mingling and said hello to some familiar faces and then made my way to a seat on the little stage. There was no assigned seating for the candidates, so we found our own. A gentleman I had not met nor seen sat down next to me. He introduced himself as James Condit, a consultant from Cincinnati. We chatted for a few minutes, and he seemed to be a nice guy. I racked my brain, trying to remember who he was but could not come up with anything.

The event started with the moderator introducing the candidates. He used a random order to call up each of us for an opening statement. The packed room felt hot due to the standing-room-only crowd as I awaited my turn. The first few candidates offered run-of-the-mill comments. They were obviously Republicans and were playing to their constituency with guns, abortion, and immigration. Then Corey Foister, the lone Democrat running, took his turn. Corey was a recent college graduate, and Baylor had said he was basically drafted into running because no one else wanted to. He was obviously uncomfortable and had not done many, if any, of these events. He spoke haltingly and without cohesion. It was painful to watch, and the look on the crowd's face said it all: *We aren't voting for you anyway.* Corey was followed by another candidate, and then they called James Condit to the podium. I expected a fairly polished speech after talking with him and also hearing that he was an attorney. I got the unexpected.

I didn't recognize Condit because he wasn't at any other events. He was the Green Party candidate. And now, he stood up to tell us about his candidacy. He started off fairly down-the-middle and maybe even leaning right. But after a few minutes, he began spewing anti-Semitic theories regarding 9/11 and a shadow Jewish government that controls everything. He railed on about highly inflated death counts for the Holocaust and that Israel was responsible for deaths in Syria that were known to be directed by their dictator Bashar al-Assad. I just stared at him and wondered how this full-blown anti-Semitic crackpot got in here, let alone on the ballot. I looked out at the audience; there was a mix of sheer shock and disbelief. The room was quiet as we all tried to get our heads around the words coming out of his mouth.

Condit finished his few minutes of hate and returned to the seat next to me. I felt the entire audience staring at him and was uncomfortable as hell being the guy next to him. I could hear a lot of murmuring, but I wasn't able to make out any words. Without thinking, I shifted my chair away from him and clanked into the guy next to me. He heard the noise and looked over at me and smiled. I was sick about that smile. One of two things occurred to me: Condit either didn't know he said anything wrong or he knew exactly what he said—and the shock value associated with it—and was proud as hell. I thought the latter, and it made me sick that he directed a smile at me. It was like the devil sitting next to you and smiling at you . . . in front of everyone.

As my mind raced to figure what just happened, I also started immediately forming a completely new set of opening remarks for my turn. There was no way I would let his remarks stand without some sort of reply. As luck would have it, Davidson was called up next. He took to the podium as I was still putting together points to make for my turn. There was a noticeable pause before he said, "I stand with Israel." The place erupted with applause, including all of us on the stage. It was a pent-up release of emotion applause and it was also meant to make a statement to Condit in the clearest terms: *You and your opinions are not welcome.*

Davidson made a few more comments and then launched into his stump speech. It really didn't matter what else he said. He killed it in that moment. Kudos to him. As much as Condit's comments and presence bothered me, I was now unhappy that Davidson beat me to the obvious reply. Through sheer luck of the draw, he drew the counterpoint slot. I gave him credit for coming up with the right line and keeping it simple and forceful. Good instincts. I was just jealous I didn't get that chance. The rest of us that followed made similar comments, but they were all forgettable.

I learned later that Condit had been at this kind of thing for a while. He didn't even like nor agree with the Green Party platform. He just used it because it was easy to get on the ballot and would be without competition, therefore making it through to the general election. He had also run under the Constitution Party and as an Independent in prior races. In this race, he would end up finishing last with 607 votes out of 28,000 cast. No surprise he was last, but who the hell are the 607 people who voted for him?

CHAPTER 22

The Homestretch

THE FINAL TWO WEEKS OF the campaign were a whirlwind. There was nonstop activity with events to attend every day. Most nights were filled with a Republican staple called Lincoln Day Dinners. Every county's GOP party had one. Although Lincoln's birthday is February 12, it seemed like every other night there was a celebration of it somewhere by the Republican Party. There wasn't a reason other than for the party's elected officials, party leadership, and funders to get together. It was typically a cocktail hour followed by dinner and then speeches by the biggest names attending. Sometimes it was a U.S. senator and other times a state-wide office holder. Occasionally, they might ask us candidates to speak as well although it always came with the standard time limit of two or three minutes.

The biggest Lincoln Day Dinner was in Butler County, home of John Boehner, and he was attending this year. Boehner had been nonexistent in the race to replace him, at least outwardly, since

Roger Reynolds dropped out early on. However, that night, he was the guest of honor and attendance was much larger than any other I attended. Tricia and I got dressed in our best and met Baylor at the hotel where it was being held.

There was a long line to check in and lots of police. There was also the all-too-obvious presence of Secret Service agents. I don't know why they just don't wear bright orange safety vests with "Secret Service" emblazoned on the back. It's impossible not to notice guys wearing black suits with black ties and shoes *and* an earpiece with squiggly wire coming out along with sunglasses at night.

We finally got through the line after showing an ID and got to the VIP reception area. The VIP reception was open for people who either gave a big donation, were already an elected official, or were running for his seat. It ended up being almost an hour of cocktails and everyone watching the door before Boehner showed up. Besides more Secret Service, he was with his wife and about six staffers, and the room suddenly lit up. There wasn't a rush to say hello to him but a concerted line did form. Tricia and I hung back as Baylor attempted to figure out the best way to approach him. It was not going to make a difference in the election but a photo-op would be fun and a reason to post something on social media.

After thirty minutes of Boehner slowly making his way around the room, I told Tricia we would get our chance soon; he was about ten feet away. I went and stood on the periphery of the people talking to him, about three rows back, with a bunch of others. Boehner was jovial, telling stories and laughing. He was clearly enjoying himself. I didn't feel like I was really getting nearer the front of the line but was close enough to notice that Boehner's wine glass was somehow always full. It certainly wasn't from his refraining to drink, as he frequently admitted to his love of red wine. The creative solution appeared right in front of me: a staffer of his regularly traded him out with a fresh glass as one was getting low. The benefits of power!

A minute later, Boehner turned away and through a back door. Some of his staff and the Secret Service guys followed him out. I thought I missed my chance and wandered back to Tricia. I told her I didn't know if he left for good and hadn't seen Baylor for a while either. I chuckled as I said it since a story Baylor had told came to mind.

A few weeks before, Baylor had told me of an event he had attended the previous year where Boehner was the headliner. Baylor was sure he wouldn't get to talk to Boehner but was determined to try. He and a friend had been talking and knew Boehner doesn't typically go very long without a cigarette. In anticipation of the famous "Boehner cigarette break," they had brought a pack of Camels (Boehner's favorite brand) and had staked out the area outside where the service entrance was located. Neither one smoked, but this was their big chance. They waited and waited, and then the door opened and Boehner stepped out with his entourage. Baylor and his friend pulled out their packs and offered Boehner a smoke. He had his own, but now it's a smoker's club and they all stood around smoking and talking.

"He's probably outside right now smoking with John!" I told Tricia.

In the end, Baylor didn't smoke with the speaker that night, but he did get us a quick introduction and a photo. The VIP hour was up soon after, and we went to find our table. The dinner and speeches were much like the other dinners, although there was not a chance for candidates to speak since Boehner was there and he had stories to tell for a while. We had fun and laughed on the way home, but it still felt like so many other nights. I didn't think I earned a vote from anyone, for sure not this late in the campaign.

Just a night of socializing, seeing, and being seen. I wondered if this was the life of a politician.

Soon thereafter, Baylor got a call from a Cincinnati television news producer who wanted to have the "leading" candidates on his morning show in a few days. It was always nice to hear I was a "leading" candidate even as we continued to see more and more Davidson ads on TV, radio, and social media. It was clear that his Club for Growth money had flowed in by the truckload. Watching TV, especially the news, was painful as Davidson ads appeared every day and night. On a few nights, there were even two spots for him during the same break between regular programming. It was obvious he had more money than he knew what to do with.

Davidson was also acting like he would win. His appearances at forums dwindled. He turned down more events than he accepted. At one of the last forums where I saw him, he even apologized to the crowd for the coming media blitz. The other candidates and I just looked at each other in disbelief.

"Did he really just say that?" I commented. We were all up on stage pouring our hearts out, telling them how hard we'd all work, how dedicated we were to our country, and how we would represent them in Washington. Davidson said a few words and then "sorry for all the money I'm about to spend"?! The trouble was, I couldn't help but believe him, especially after Club for Growth prevented us from raising money from Aegis, the Koch brothers group, and others.

True to his recent form, Davidson declined the invitation to be on the morning TV news program, which opened up a spot for another. It ended up being me, Beagle, Winteregg, and White (the late entry). The morning of the show, I met Baylor at the TV station and we went in to get ready. It was not really much of a forum but really a two-minute commercial. The anchor sat in the middle of five barstools, introduced us all, and then asked one question to each of us. It was over quickly and was another episode that left me wondering what difference it would make. In any case, I kept that thought to myself (as I always did) and walked out with Baylor.

As we walked into the parking lot, J.D. Winteregg caught up with us. He wanted to talk. As we stood in a circle with his campaign manager also present, he got right to the point. He had talked to Kevin White, and they had an idea. Before he started in with his idea, he relayed that White was angry that he was not invited to this morning's event until the last minute to replace Davidson. Of course, this was the same Kevin White who was sure he won every forum and was one of the leaders. Winteregg appeared to be unsettled as well but got on with his idea. With time running out, Winteregg and White wanted me to join them in a joint press conference. There, we would lay out where Davidson got all the outside money he was spending on advertising. We would all claim outsiders were trying to buy "our" election. The theory was that the press would run with this and possibly it would kill Davidson's momentum and maybe his chances to win.

Baylor and I were nodding like we were listening and considering his "big" idea. I was pretty sure Baylor was also thinking the same thing I was. All of the top contenders in this race had received money from outside the district and outside the state. Maybe not Winteregg and White, but Beagle, Derickson, and I had all received "outside" contributions to our campaigns. Winteregg said he and White were ready to do this in a few days. They just wanted me to join them. The "more the merrier" was the logic. Baylor and I promised to get back with him after we chatted about the idea.

It only took about twenty minutes of discussion on the way home to decide we were not going to participate. There really wasn't an upside, and complaining about another candidate had never been my thing. Starting it now would look like three grown men whining about their competitor who raised more money than them. No thanks. Baylor called Winteregg later the next day and let him know.

Winteregg and White did go ahead with their press conference. From what we heard, it was sparsely attended and barely got any mentions in the press. It was a nonevent for a lot of reasons. Among the biggest: outside money is old news and there was no smoking gun as to where this money came from. That's the beauty/problem with Super PACs and especially Club for Growth's model of fundraising. The other problem was that the three top contenders with Davidson, namely me, Beagle, and Derickson, were not there. So, at best, this was coming from two candidates whom no one expected to win.

There was one other reason I did not want to be a part of this press conference. For the last couple of weeks, I had had several conversations with an executive at one of the largest companies in my industry. I had let him know about the Davidson money and asked him if there was any way to raise significant funds quickly to match this effort. His lone idea was to ask the only person in our industry who was capable of making a sizeable contribution on his own that would make a difference. He was going to ask for a $1 million donation from one of the most successful businessmen in our industry. The logic seemed simple. The individual, who was a billionaire, could afford it.

The gentleman he was asking also knew me, at least some, and came to my event in Las Vegas. He and his son had already made the maximum donations possible, which was $2,700. He was known to be politically interested and could make this donation to my Super PAC.

This was my Hail Mary. The first conversations between the executive and the billionaire were reported to go well, meaning he didn't say "no." Follow-up messaging indicated he was still thinking about it, but the final answer was "no." It was a disappointment but certainly understandable. I never did hear an explanation, but I appreciated his consideration of the request. To even think about it, whether for real or not, seemed like a huge deal to me. Maybe the answer would have been different had I started the campaign months earlier and made the request then. Even as a novice political campaigner, I don't think asking for a lot of money weeks before an election makes a lot of sense.

CHAPTER 23

Robo Nonsense

TOWARD THE END OF THE campaign, we had a few final choices about how to spend our dwindling funds. Mark suggested a major portion of the spend go toward a robocall effort. This meant hiring a firm to do a large set of calls with a prerecorded message. He thought a combination of Tricia and I talking about the race directed at a specific set of likely Republican primary voters could have an impact on the undecideds. Although he wasn't sure of how big the undecideds were as a subset of all voters, he felt it was potentially large and could pay off if done within a week of the election. He shared a POLITICO Pro poll that showed it could be as high as 60 percent.

Mark wrote a script, and Tricia and I read through it and liked what he wrote. It was to the point on the issues but also had a lighthearted touch with Tricia. According to Mark, including Tricia would appeal to female voters and soften my tougher image. We recorded it in Tricia's studio at our house where she did professional recordings (she was a voiceover talent for years). Her help in recording and coaching me helped, and we had it done quickly. Now, it was up to Mark to get the "robo" guys to set it up.

The calls were due to be made over one night between 6:00 p.m. and 8:00 p.m. We wouldn't really know the results other than calls made, calls answered, and some sort of vague amount of time before the call ended which indicates if they listened.

It was about 6:30 p.m. the night of the calls when we started getting comments on social media and my website. Apparently, a few people were getting multiple calls. This was disconcerting. *Maybe it's just a glitch*, I thought in the moment. Then the complaints increased. By the next morning, there had been several dozen posts and comments about the harassing nature of the calls. Some people got called repeatedly and were quite upset. Needless to say, I was upset as well.

I talked a few times with Baylor to try to judge the extent of the problem. Mark was on the phone with the vendor trying to figure out the same. I told Baylor that we needed to respond individually to each complaint, as if it came from me personally, and apologize. I talked to Mark, and he still had no better information on how often this might have happened. Some glitch with the software was all he got. The crappy answers only made me more irate. I asked Mark what they were going to do about it. Then, I asked what *he* was going to do about it.

In trying to figure out the potential impact, the vendor sent us some statistics. Here's what they looked like:

Total Calls Scheduled	23,916
Total Calls with Verified Return	19,815
Total Calls with Human Answer	7,612 (38%)
Total Calls with Machine Answer	9,696 (49%)
Total Calls with Message Delivery	2,507 (13%)
Average Call Time with Human Answer	53 seconds
# of Human Answer Less than 30 seconds	3,607
# of Human Answer More than 30 seconds	4,005

All this boiled down means the calls reached just shy of 8,000 Republican voters who listened on average for 53 seconds. It was not a terrible effort, given that we were expecting 125,000 voters to cast their ballots, but we still didn't know whether to believe the numbers or how many of the calls were repeated.

In the end, our apologies to the people who complained helped some. Many responded, with some saying they weren't going to let it affect their vote and others who were just plain pissed off. The vendor offered to redo another night for free, to which I said, "Hell no." Mark offered to pay for it out of his own pocket, which wasn't going to solve anything. It was a disaster, and we never knew its magnitude, but we hoped it was minimal. It was a frustrating end to our campaign spending and left a bitter taste in my mouth. Old school was not the way to go.

CHAPTER 24

The Final Days

I HAD JUST FINISHED MY last candidate forum on the Thursday before election day and felt like I was genuinely comfortable in these settings. The responses after the forums had been getting steadily more positive and more numerous. After this last one, the local county engineer and county treasurer had both made their way through the crowd to congratulate me and said, "You're the only real candidate we heard tonight." Tricia and I took extra time afterward to talk to as many people as we could. I particularly wanted to savor the experience, because I wasn't sure there would ever be another candidate forum for me.

It was abundantly clear that Davidson's money had shown up in spades. He was on TV, radio, newspapers, billboards, and everywhere on social media. No one else came close to the exposure he was generating. In fact, it was as if no one else was even making an appearance on any media. Davidson was spending so much money that even my friends said they couldn't turn on a TV, radio, or computer without getting bombarded by him. It was so much money that they were even running back-to-back TV ads during primetime on network stations.

While I rarely spoke in specific terms about the impact of all this spending, I knew I was not going to win. I held out the slightest hope—one of those "miracles do happen" kind of hopes—that maybe there was a chance, but I knew it was not rational. Tricia never said a thing about it other than mentioning the sheer volume of Davidson ads. Baylor and Mark were the same way. Not speaking openly about what we all knew made it easier to soldier on. And it made it more enjoyable to go to that last forum and finish up the last days as strongly as we had started this journey.

The last weekend would be spent door knocking, along with a virtual town hall meeting done on Facebook Live on Sunday night. The door knocks Saturday and Sunday included Tricia and me and several diehard volunteers. We started at our usual time and enjoyed ourselves, although there was some melancholy lurking below the surface. Tricia was always so upbeat that we found ourselves doing a lot of smiling and holding hands between houses.

Door knocks this late had evolved a bit. There were a few honest replies about supporting other candidates and also many more people who had heard of me. We enjoyed those the most. At one house, another encounter with a big dog had us leaving a flyer on the door handle and walking down the driveway. We got halfway to the next house when we heard a man's voice behind us. He yelled "Hey, Jim Spurlino! I love your stuff, and I'm voting for you!" It was the owner of the big dog, and he was waving the flyer we left. I yelled back "Thank you!" and waved. Tricia yelled "Yay!" and waved too. I reached out and found her hand and we started walking to the next house, both of us with big smiles and a little extra zip in our step.

The same day, Baylor forwarded me an email that arrived via the campaign's website. The message had a subject line of "No Need to Respond BUT . . ." It read: "I just placed my absentee ballot for you because of the Christian stand you seem to have and what was written on your site. I totally believe that you were threatened and I am so sorry you and your family have had to endure that. I just wanted to remind you that Jesus is in charge! He will support the one who supports HIM! Put Him first in ALL things, and He will raise up the leaders. He's allowed the Nation to be under extreme evil for many years for a reason—perhaps Christians will 'WAKE UP' now! Just a word of encouragement but also a reminder: we do NOTHING on our own, if God puts you in this position, it is ALL for His glory! Never forget to give Him the glory! Best Wishes, Donna Marie".

I forwarded it to Tricia, and she called me. We both agreed that it was so nice of her to take the time to send the note. There were some folks out on the campaign trail who we were fortunate enough to meet and get to know for a short time. And then, there were some like her who we never met but feel lucky and blessed to have received her vote and her message. Thanks, Donna Marie. And amen.

Baylor came over about 5:00 p.m. on Sunday to set up for the Facebook Live event. It had been publicized on Facebook and all my other social media accounts. The plan was for Baylor to act as host and we would take written questions and calls. We sat down at our kitchen table going over the plan as Tricia fiddled with the lighting.

We got started right on time, and there was a solid flow of people waiting to ask questions as well as written ones piling up online. Baylor introduced me, and I gave a few remarks along with a heartfelt "thanks" for everyone who was listening and watching. We were on for an hour, and the questions were all ones I had heard and answered before. However, it felt different because no one was timing me to make sure my answers didn't go over forty-five seconds. Also, Baylor and I had good chemistry, and I think it came off as a folksy chat with a friend. I'm guessing most of those who attended or listened were supporters or at least leaning that way. It was a perfect cap to all the forums and events I had done.

Monday, the day before the election, was spent without any formal events. It was almost too quiet for me. My phone rang the same amount, but it was mostly friends wishing me well or just checking to see how I was doing. Most would ask what I thought the outcome of the election would be, to which I answered that I was hopeful. I still wasn't talking much about the insurmountable money and odds we faced.

Baylor called several times. Some reporters wanted to know where I would be on election day when the results starting coming in. He talked about getting a hotel conference room and inviting supporters. I wasn't much into having a wake. I told him Tricia and I would just be home, watching TV there, and that he was welcome to join us. As for the media, they didn't need to know where I was going to be, and they could call Baylor if they wanted anything.

Tuesday, March 15, 2016, came like any other day, except it was obviously much more. I got up like usual, and Tricia and I got in the car for the ten-minute drive to our polling place. The church we voted at was not very busy, and we cast our votes. There was no fanfare or celebrating, and we were back in the car in less than ten minutes. We drove home, and I told her I was going to my office. I didn't know what else to do, and I sure couldn't sit around the house waiting for the inevitable.

I plowed through my workday and actually made progress getting caught up after three months of part-time working. I headed home about 5:00 p.m. and got lots of words of support from everyone in the office. Besides Lou and Gary, there were lots and lots of people at work who helped my campaign in one way or the other. Everyone was so supportive and hearing their last encouraging words before I left made me very proud to have them all as employees and friends.

I was home for a bit before Baylor arrived. He brought James with him, our faithful Miami University supporter and part-time campaign employee. Tricia and our kids were all home and helping prepare food to munch on throughout what would be a long night. I sat in my office and could not resist making a guess what the outcome would be. I knew Davidson would win and thought Beagle or Derickson would follow. I was hoping to beat one or both of them and come in second, but I knew that fourth was likely and I'd be happy to hang onto that spot.

We all ate and drank for several hours until the TV started giving us some results. Of course, the big news was the Republican primary for president, but we made sure to have local news on where they run local election results and sometimes have that banner at the bottom of the screen too. The initial results, with less than 10 percent of the precincts reporting, were indicative of the rest of the night. It forecasted Davidson on top followed by Derickson, Beagle, and me.

As more and more precincts reported, the results did not change, and it was all but official by 9:00 p.m. for my race. The result was:

Davidson	33%
Derickson	24%
Beagle	20%
Spurlino	7%

Everyone else was less than 4 percent. It really wasn't very close, considering Derickson and Beagle began with significant name recognition throughout the district. I was fairly disappointed with 7 percent, but the numbers above me weren't going to change, and the eleven candidates below me split the remaining 17 percent, so the math seemed logical.

Voter turnout in an Ohio primary is difficult to estimate due the state's open primary system. This system doesn't require registration with a political party to vote in a primary. You simply ask for the ballot of your choice, either Republican or Democratic, and then cast your vote. It, in turn, acts as a de facto registration of your affiliation. We do know the official turnout as recorded by the Ohio Secretary of State was about 28 percent of eligible voters.

Mark called, and we talked briefly. There wasn't much to say at that point. He had kind words and wished me well. We promised to stay in touch. I got off that call, somewhat as if that was the final and official word, and walked into the other room where Baylor was. He looked dejected, as if he'd just gotten the news even though he knew what the outcome was going to be. I'll never forget him looking at me and asking if I wanted him to leave. Now I felt bad.

"Of course not," I replied. We needed a drink. I had him follow me to our bar, and I filled two glasses with ice and then bourbon all the way to the brim. "Let's go sit outside," I said. We walked out to our back porch and sat down. I pulled out some cigarettes, and we both lit one followed by long sips of bourbon.

I told him what an awesome job he had done and how much Tricia and I appreciated all his efforts. He had been the complete professional and worked his butt off nonstop for more than three months. I had come to not only appreciate his work but also admire how smart and tactical he really was. But far and away the most important thing, I told him, was that he had become a friend to Tricia and I and that would never change.

Baylor looked relieved although still taken with disappointment. He took another big sip and said, "When you came in the room after talking to Mark, I wasn't sure if you were going to punch me or throw me out." We both laughed. I knew he was being honest. I assured him that neither of those crossed my mind, and I felt bad that I hadn't raised more money and started my campaign far earlier. "It would have given us a fighting chance," I said, very much believing it but still not sure we could have won.

We talked more and laughed more and generally released all our pent-up emotions and energy. Another bourbon and more cigarettes helped too. It was close to 11:00 p.m. when we finally went inside and Baylor said his goodbyes. Tricia gave him a big hug and told him how much he meant to us. It all came to a rather quiet end as Baylor walked down our sidewalk to his car.

Tricia and I were the only ones left awake, and so we cleaned up and then called it a night. I remember Tricia commenting on how relieved I looked. She said she knew I was ready for this all to be over and that I was anxious to get on with our lives as we knew and loved them before the campaign. We went to bed without turning on the TV again, and I slept soundly. I guess it is possible to be disappointed and relieved at the same time.

CHAPTER 25

Lessons Learned

I LEARNED A LOT ABOUT the art of politics during my campaign. Some of it was encouraging, but a fair amount of it was disheartening. The biggest takeaway was that money buys elections, and it often has nothing to do with support in your district or who you really are. This is not just my experience. In all House races during the past twenty years, the candidate who spent more money has won more than 90 percent of the time.[15] Yes, those are general election figures, but I suspect the figures are not that different for primaries. In fact, I'd bet that the winning percentages in primaries are even higher for the candidate who spends the most, since turnout is lower. And those figures don't even account for Super PACs, which probably skew the winning percentages even higher.

In my campaign, the clearest evidence of money's influence stemmed from Warren Davidson winning the primary—and doing so by such a large margin. While he is a decent person and had a record of public service and a business background, there was not much to distinguish him from the other candidates. He was not more conservative, he was not better in debates, and he did not run sharper ads. He simply had a lot more money. Had I had his money advantage, I'm confident I would have won. But I also think if Derickson or Beagle had the money advantage, one of them would have prevailed.

The backdrop to Davidson securing so much funding was that John Boehner and Jim Jordan had been feuding for several years before Boehner resigned. The resignation represented an opportunity for Jordan to increase the size of his Freedom Caucus and stick a needle in Boehner on his way out. There is no question that Jordan handpicked Davidson.

Davidson did pledge to join the Freedom Caucus, and based on the source of the funding, it appears Jordan did bring in a ton of outside money to put Davidson on top. It is not much more complicated than that. The Club for Growth, their associates, and all the outsiders enabled Davidson to rapidly achieve a level of name recognition that surpassed all of his opponents. He knew he was going to sail ahead of the pack and even told an audience at one forum that he was about to start flooding the media with commercials and wanted to apologize in advance. I can only imagine what Jordan and the Club for Growth folks told him that led to that odd proclamation.

With or without Davidson's outside money and knowing now what I didn't know then, I would have approached the race for Boehner's seat differently. Perhaps most importantly, I would have started much earlier. The decision to get in should have been within a week or two of Boehner announcing his resignation. This would have afforded me more time to raise money and possibly thwart or at least slow down the surge of outside money that went to Davidson.

I would have also been truer to my own positions and not allowed Mark to push me uncomfortably to the right. In the end, this was my decision, so I'll own it, but I think a center-right candidate had just as much chance to win as did a far-right candidate. In the end, command of the issues and honest articulation of them could have been a tiebreaker, if the money was equal, and I knew I had the edge there.

I get asked all the time whether I regretted running or would run again. The answers to both are "no." I have no regrets because I did enjoy the experience and believe I learned a lot from it. I met many wonderful people who live in the district and many others who sent me campaign donations because they believed in me. And I learned a lot about our political system, even if it was not all good.

I don't think I would run again for several reasons. First, I'm not sure I want to put my family through the experience again. My wife was terrific, and the kids never complained, but I know my candidacy took a toll on them. Second, I wouldn't run unless I was confident that enough money could be raised to be competitive. I know more now about that equation and realize it would be a significantly higher amount, taking more time and effort than when I ran the first time. Third, I would not want to get elected by way of outside money that had no meaningful connection to me. Yes, I had a Super PAC, but I knew the donors and they knew me. I had money donated from people outside the district, but, again, I knew them and they knew me. There is not an amount of money that would convince me to follow a caucus or direction blindly in order to get elected.

As much as I enjoyed the campaign experience, I also suspect that there are countless capable people who would make fine members of the House, in either party, but don't want to subject themselves to everything that comes with being a candidate. Having to ask for money all the time is very unpleasant, and I doubt there's any correlation between being a good fundraiser and being an effective congressman. There's also all the scrutiny—of a candidate's finances and personal life—that so often emerges, and not in a flattering (or accurate) way. All of these downsides only get magnified once you're in office, and it comes with nonstop travel between the district and Washington. Just about any sane person would survey the situation and ask, "Why would I want to do that?"

I am occasionally asked how I think Davidson is doing as a congressman. The answer is that I'm not sure. He was reelected in 2018 and 2020, so maybe that's the answer. But to me, his representation, or more important his service, has been lacking.

My comments are not driven by animosity or sour grapes. Later, I lay out what I think matters most in a representative. He just doesn't tick any of those boxes. He's not doing the basics of advocating for what's best for the district and advocating for what's best for our country. Also, I haven't seen evidence of him authoring, sponsoring, or co-sponsoring meaningful legislation or even trying to get important legislation passed. That's the minimum basic responsibility of a congressman to me.

He made national headlines in January 2022 when commenting, via Twitter, on Washington, DC, requiring people to show proof of vaccination when entering different kinds of business establishments. One of his tweets read: "This has been done before. #DoNotComply," and it included an image of a Nazi document with a swastika. He then sent another tweet that read: "Let's recall that the Nazis dehumanized Jewish people before segregating them, segregated them before imprisoning them, imprisoned them before enslaving them, and enslaved them before massacring them."[16]

His inflammatory comments—which were criticized by Jewish organizations and Jewish House members—were ironic given the episode I describe earlier, in which he responded to anti-Semitic rhetoric uttered at a candidate forum by declaring: "I stand with Israel." (I don't think Davidson meant to be offensive to Jews, but rather let his zealous opposition to vaccine mandates get the best of him.)

Davidson was also in the news in 2021 for failing to comply with a federal law requiring members of Congress to disclose, within forty-five days, any stock market transition valued at more than $1,000. An outside advocacy group publicized that he had sold stock worth between $50,000 and $100,000 but had not disclosed it.[17] Notably, Davidson is a member of the House Financial Services Committee and has an MBA from Notre Dame. Had any Democrat (or Republican opponent) failed to report such a transaction, Davidson would have denounced them for it.

I'll never challenge him for his seat, so this discussion is not self-serving. I just don't see him getting a passing grade in any of these situations. The only consolation is that he has plenty of company among his 434 brothers and sisters in the House.

What would I have been like as a congressman? I don't know really. It's hard to imagine. You have aspirations and ideals, but it's hard to tell. I do know that I would have either made a difference or not run for reelection. I didn't aspire to be another Speaker of the House like Boehner, but I would not have wasted my time or my constituents' votes by not making a difference. That's why I ran, and that's how I would have served.

CHAPTER 26

Baylor

DURING MY RUN FOR OFFICE, Baylor became more than just my campaign manager. Tricia and I valued his hard work, integrity, and political acumen, while also coming to see him as a friend. His dedication and efforts were impressive and revealed the true nature of his spirit. Tricia even said that she thought Baylor took my loss harder than me. We kept in touch regularly and were rooting for him to find the best opportunity in his next job.

He has had a very successful and productive career since my campaign. I've told him often that he owes it all to me—for losing and having to fire him. After a short time of pondering his next job after my loss, he was contacted by Corey Lewandowski who was then Trump's campaign manager. Corey had been Baylor's boss's boss at Americans for Prosperity (AFP), and they knew each other some.

Corey offered Baylor a job on the Trump campaign working out of Trump Tower in New York City. Baylor called me and we chatted about the opportunity. I think he saw it as a great opportunity to work on a presidential campaign. He packed his bags and began his next assignment.

I continued to talk to him regularly but not as often. He was often flying with or ahead of Trump to campaign stops across the country. We saw Baylor a few weeks before the general election, and he was upbeat. We attended a Trump rally in Wilmington, Ohio, with the real intent to just see Baylor. We chatted while waiting for Trump to arrive, and he told us that inside the Trump campaign there was real optimism. He said they had tangible polling evidence that Trump could win, although almost all the media gave him no chance. I didn't believe him, but we all know what happened.

After Trump's win, Baylor was given the chance to join the administration. The job wasn't really clear, but he was given a choice of departments. He chose Treasury and became the liaison to the White House. After a few years, he was promoted to deputy chief of staff to Secretary of the Treasury Steven Mnuchin. In this position, he worked closely with the secretary on some of our nation's most important issues. It was quite a trajectory from my campaign manager to deputy chief of staff to the secretary of treasury.

Baylor left government work on Trump's last day in office. He now works as director of business operations at BitGo, an institutional digital asset company based in Palo Alto, California. Best of all, Tricia and I still consider him a close friend.

CHAPTER 27

The Numbers

I'M A BIT OF A math nerd and often feel the need to create a spreadsheet for anything with numbers. Some months after I lost the election, the Federal Election Commission (FEC) released final numbers on my race's campaign financing, and I couldn't help but review the figures. There weren't many surprises in the outcome, but the numbers do reveal a few interesting things. One caveat when looking at my numbers: I used the FEC numbers along withopensecrets.org for outside spending. The numbers are what are reported, and, in the case of the FEC, how they ask for it. See the next page for my spreadsheet:

Ohio Congressional District 8

REPUBLICAN PRIMARY

March 15, 2016

Candidate	Warren Davidson	Tim Derickson	Bill Beagle	Jim Spurlino	J.D. Winteregg	Scott George	Terri King	Kevin White	Michael Smith	John Robbins	Matt Ashworth	Eric Haemmerle	George Wooley	Ed Meer	Joe Matvey	Total	% of Total
Finished	1	2	3	4	5	6	7	8	9	10	11	12	13	14	15		
Age	46	55	51	52	33	48	55	51	44	77	48	43	61	39	55		
Occupation	Businessman	Politician	Politician	Businessman	Farm Worker	Consultant	Attorney	Pilot	Un-employed	Retired	Under-writer	Teacher	Businessman	Factory Work	Accountant		
Other	Veteran	State Rep	State Senate		Previously ran		Previously ran	Veteran	Banker	Steel-worker			Mailman	Veteran			
County	Miami	Butler	Miami	Outside	Miami	Miami	Butler	Clark	Outside	Butler	Butler	Butler	Miami	Butler	Butler		
Votes	43,602	32,578	26,424	9,253	5,316	3,069	2,879	2,314	1,995	1,560	1,490	1,345	1,008	609	566	$134,008	28%
Registered Voters	33%	24%	20%	7%	4%	2%	2%	2%	1%	1%	1%	1%	1%	0.5%	0.4%		
Total Raised	$977,809	$314,412	$501,672	$351,007	$95,628	$6,615	$-	$20,000	$-	$-	$-	$-	$-	$-	$2,583	$2,269,726	
Individual	$498,569	$229,128	$257,262	$151,007	$73,571	$6,615	$-	$3,100	$-	$-	$-	$-	$-	$-	$-	$1,219,252	54%
Committee	$216,209	$65,884	$52,000	$35,500	$-	$-	$-	$-	$-	$-	$-	$-	$-	$-	$-	$369,593	16%
Personal Loans	$250,000	$20,000	$191,000	$200,000	$9,100	$-	$-	$16,900	$-	$-	$-	$-	$-	$-	$2,583	$689,583	30%
Campaign Spent	$866,937	$305,362	$501,672	$351,007	$96,528	$6,615	$-	$19,983	$-	$-	$-	$-	$-	$-	$2,583	$2,150,687	47%
Outside Spending	$1,424,232	$973,277	$-	$-	$-	$-	$-	$-	$-	$-	$-	$-	$-	$-	$-	$2,397,509	53%
Total Spent	$2,291,169	$1,278,639	$501,672	$351,007	$96,528	$6,615	$-	$19,983	$-	$-	$-	$-	$-	$-	$2,583	$4,548,196	
% of Total Spent	50%	28%	11%	8%	2%	0%	0%	0%	0%	0%	0%	0%	0%	0%	0%		
Outside Opposed (not in calculations)	$293,349	$32,601	$96,688	$-	$-	$-	$-	$-	$-	$-	$-	$-	$-	$-	$-	$422,638	
$ spent per vote	$52.55	$39.25	$18.99	$37.93	$18.16	$2.16	$-	$8.64	$-	$-	$-	$-	$-	$-	$4.56	$33.94	
Notable Outside																	
Club for Growth	$1,133,765																
Right Way Initiative		$703,486															

If nothing else changed, how much more money to win?

	Terri King	Kevin White	Michael Smith
Votes needed	34,349	34,349	34,349
Cost	$52.55	$37.93	$37.93
	$1,804,948	to	$1,303,009

What's most revealing is that Davidson raised and spent almost as much as the other fourteen candidates combined, and his outside spending was over 69 percent of his total. As I've said earlier, this spending decided the race. Let's dive a little deeper into his numbers because there is more to be learned. The significant ones are:

Campaign Raised: $977,809 (or $727,809 excluding his personal loan)

That's a big amount and quite a bit more than anyone else. How was a first-timer able to do this? Was he just more popular? While it's hard to know for sure, the likely true answer is that this is another indication of the influence of Jim Jordan and the Club for Growth. Why? Because when they want to support a candidate, they ask their large network of wealthy associates to send donations directly to a candidate's campaign. You could guess that Davidson probably didn't raise much more on his own than I—the other first-timer—did, therefore the Club for Growth portion might be something like $250,000 just to his campaign. When you look at the reports, you also see donors like FreedomWorks, House Freedom Fund, Senate Conservatives Fund, and, yes, Jim Jordan for Congress.

Outside Spending: $1,424,232

Of this total, Club for Growth contributed $1,133,765 or 80 percent. This alone was 25 percent of the total spending by all of the primary candidates.

Outside Opposed: $293,349

This was money spent by Derickson supporters. Derickson, who finished second, clearly recognized that Davidson was his primary competitor.

Some other interesting figures include the outside money spent opposing Derickson and Beagle. This was primarily spent by my Super PAC in the mistaken belief that these two were my main rivals. It was good logic early in the campaign, but once the Davidson outside money was apparent, then it only helped him get elected. In fact, one night after a forum he made his way over to chat and said, "Thanks for the help." I looked at him quizzically, and he went on to explain flyers that were mailed attacking Beagle and Derickson and paid for by "Americans for Concrete Solutions." It wasn't too hard to figure out, but I had no idea.

Seven of the fifteen candidates didn't spend a dime, and it showed with all but one receiving about 1 percent of the total votes. The only outlier in this group was Terri King, a local attorney who had run for public office twice before and therefore had some name recognition. Three others spent $20,000 or less, leaving only five candidates who spent $96,000 or more. And, in total, the candidates spent $4.3 million for 134,000 votes for a rate of $32 per vote.

One row on the spreadsheet shows dollars spent for each vote. Beagle and Winteregg did the best, at about $18–$19 per vote. For Beagle, this was due to having run for office successfully twice before in a state senate district that covered much of the district. For Winteregg, it likely came from running against Boehner in the 2014 primary and having name recognition from that experience. Derickson and I were next, spending $38–$40 per vote, and Davidson was the most with a per vote spend of $53.

Another row in the spreadsheet calculates how much more money I needed to raise to pull even with Davidson. Using my rate per vote and his higher rate per vote, it came out to $1.3 million–$1.4 million. It made me realize that I was that close but also that far. Maybe the billionaire industry friend could have put me over the top, or maybe I just needed to have started raising money earlier. In any case, these are just numbers and guesses and certainly don't account for the candidates themselves.

CHAPTER 28

Post-Campaign
Public Service

MY POST-CAMPAIGN LIFE WAS CERTAINLY less political than it had been, but the political side that did exist seemed to take on a whole new dimension. Almost immediately, it seemed like everyone I knew assumed I was an expert on all things political. Prior to running for Congress, I would have the same conversations about politics as any group of friends might have. Now, I was seen as having insights no one else did. Topics would come up, and I would always get asked my opinion, and my opinion always seemed to carry a lot of weight. I also noticed that people would bring up political topics more often and ask what I thought about them.

The funny thing is that, yes, I was now a little more informed about political topics but not *that* much more than before I ran for Congress. I was well-informed before and could speak intelligently about a lot of political issues, but now I was an anointed expert, a scholar with worldly wisdom. It was an intriguing overnight change. It is also interesting to note that it continues to this day. It hasn't diminished one bit. I guess, if anything, it makes me stay on top of issues and topics since I am still asked a lot about is going on in the political world regularly. I don't want to let anyone down!

The other related thing is that I seemed to get a little more respect and responsiveness from elected officials. They became quicker to respond or there would be an extra few minutes of conversation. It wasn't as significant a change as with my friends and acquaintances, but it was detectable.

I was also getting more requests from Washington to attend meetings, and I received two offers to be considered for positions in the federal government. Those were completely new and out of left field for me. While I had been active in advocating for early childhood matters for years, which had brought me to Washington several times a year for the last decade, I almost immediately started getting these higher profile invitations. It started soon after the election hype died down and Trump was sworn in.

In April 2017, the Speaker of the House Paul Ryan was putting together six task forces on different policy issues. One of the task forces was focused, at least in part, on early childhood issues. It was named "Poverty, Opportunity, and Upward Mobility." The congressional members of the task force were four House committee chairs, including the powerful chair of Ways and Means. I was asked whether I would assist in writing a policy brief for the task force and participate in meetings in DC with senior staff. I was happy to do this and looked forward to the important work this could entail. In the end, this amounted to more emails and input than meetings and full policy review. Still, it seemed like a start to something more.

This was followed by several meetings over the next twelve months or so with staff from various House and Senate committees. This included the House Committee on Ways and Means, House Committee on Education and Labor, House Budget Committee, Senate HELP Committee, and Senate Finance Committee as well as meetings with staff from numerous House and Senate members. All of these conversations revolved around early childhood issues and made me greatly appreciate the hard work and dedication of the professional staff of the standing committees as well as each legislators' staff. I could tell firsthand how serious they all took the U.S. government's work. I also took pride in hearing the comments made about me by one meeting organizer. He suggested a think tank "translate the [research] into policy action on the Hill by bringing the author and a 'real person' up [there] so we can talk about the research, what it means, and how it can fit into what we're doing." The "real person" he referred to was me. It was similar to how I felt being called "normal" on the campaign trail—a great compliment.

In September 2017 I was invited to attend an "Early Childhood Listening Session" at the Department of Health and Human Services (HHS). It was hosted by Steve Wagner, the assistant secretary/ principal deputy assistant secretary of HHS who was leading the Administration for Children and Families (ACF). ACF manages sixty programs and has a $62 billion budget. Their largest programs include Temporary Assistance for Needy Families (TANF), Head Start, foster care, childcare, and child support enforcement. The agenda for the meeting indicated I was one of five invitees who were meeting with the leadership of ACF.

The meeting was very interesting, and I was impressed with their leadership team. It was a good exchange of ideas, and they did indeed listen. I hate to admit I was surprised at that, but I think most Americans don't expect our government to listen. Kudos to these folks. At the end of the meeting, Assistant Secretary Wagner asked each of us if we had any closing remarks. We went around the table, and I was close to last. I said I didn't have any additional remarks, but I did have a question. "If ACF didn't exist today and Congress appropriated to you your entire budget now, what would you do with it? Would you recreate exactly what you have today?" I asked. There were audible nos including from Wagner. I kept going: "If not, then what would you do? And why isn't that where to start? Isn't that the direction and strategy that should be undertaken?" This got a lot of heads shaking up and down.

After the meeting broke up, there was some brief chitchat, but clearly the ACF folks had more on their calendars for the day and most people filed out. Wagner was one of the last, and he stopped and thanked me for my time. He said he especially liked the candor and directness of my comments. Another handshake and we all headed out. I rode the elevator down and looked at my phone. Almost three hours had passed very quickly, and I was still energized. It was great to have a serious conversation about issues important to me with people who just might do something about it.

A week passed, and I sent Wagner some thoughts about the meeting and what I meant by my closing remarks. The email was a bit lengthy, but I had taken my own question seriously and wanted to provide some detail, even if at a high level. Here is what I sent:

> *I have thought often about writing to you following the meeting at ACF. I do think that reimagining what and how ACF conducts its work is important to do and that was verified by the ACF leadership at the meeting. I am not sure I am in the best position*

to make suggestions without their knowledge and experience but here are a few thoughts:

My sense is that ACF has all the information within itself to re-imagine their work. How they go about this is fairly straightforward as with any problem-solving exercise such as 1) Define the problem/issue/goal, 2) Identify potential solutions, 3) Evaluate potential solutions, 4) Select solutions, 5) Design new system including evaluation and monitoring, and 6) Implement. I think utilizing both internal and external resources will yield the best results.

Some thoughts on what might be overarching themes:

A) Increase/maximize block granting to states—although most non-entitlement health and social programs (TANF, child care, child welfare, maternal and child health, social services, etc.) were block granted in the eighties and nineties, there is more to do.

B) Decrease ACF-direct oversight of programs and focus on protecting federal investment from misuse and protect families from weak state administration. Standards, quality, and outcomes developed and overseen by ACF should be their focus.

C) Increase and strengthen research to align with program goals and inform and drive program initiatives. A portion of funds could also be allocated to states for work in QI and evaluation research. As an example, The MCH block grant in health has this type of funding for "projects of national significance."

D) Increase the number and amount of state matches. This makes our dollars go further and promotes states' self-interest in fiscal responsibility. There should, however, be limits so as not to disadvantage poorer states.

E) Emphasize outcome-based programming and funding rather than compliance-based. This should also be at the heart of the accountability component woven throughout ACF. An example from my own experience: Every Child Succeeds runs an Early Head Start program in Cincinnati. As chairman of the board, I was required to sign and certify petty cash expenditures every month for the EHS program. Nothing about the families, staff, outcomes, etc. This is just an example of how compliance has overtaken common sense.

F) Maintain maximum flexibility for state implementation of their programs (while continuing standards, accountability, etc.). Standards are necessary, good, and needed but if not balanced with flexibility, then states lose the ability to address their unique and regional issues for the maximum benefit of their population.

G) Develop incentives for innovation with an emphasis on usefulness of this work. Ability to replicate, scale, meet unmet needs, and portability are critical. The "projects of national significance" are relevant here too.

H) Direct more resources and funding to earlier ages including prenatal. We won't make real sustainable progress without starting at the very earliest we can. This is also where research can inform us as to providing for larger systems of health and development and a real continuum of services.

I) Consider a structure and process similar to MIECHV where programs/models are approved and then states choose what is best for them. ACF should monitor and promote the appropriateness and fiscal responsibility of states' selection of programming. This acknowledges that states do a reasonable job with their MIECHV funds but often serve only pockets of at-risk populations. The "larger systems" mentioned above need to be addressed or developed where service becomes siloed.

J) Include in design and work throughout this process the resources for ACF to conduct inter-agency and inter-departmental work. In the future, I'd think it is possible that our at-risk families could be best served by a federal agency funded by multiple departments to address their needs in the most effective and efficient manner. Might be a much bigger concept for later exploration.

I hope all this makes some sense and I am certainly interested in your thoughts on it.

I know the email was lengthy to include here, but I wanted to give a sense of the conversations I was having. They were neither run-of-the-mill nor superficial. My question and the follow-up email apparently got some attention. I soon received an email from a policy researcher at a DC think tank who asked if I was interested in heading the Office of Head Start. At the time, it had a $9.2 billion annual budget, with programs in every congressional district in the country. I was flabbergasted and honored to even be considered. This was followed by several conversations and then a call from Assistant Secretary Wagner. He wanted to meet for dinner and talk about it. And he would come to my hometown, Dayton, Ohio, to do it.

I was nervous and excited at the same time, but I was happy to meet. Now, I had to have a similar conversation with my wife as I had had prior to running for Congress. "What do you think about moving to DC?" I asked like it was a conversation about where to eat dinner. We talked on and off for a few days, and Tricia was as supportive as ever, if that's what I wanted to do.

I picked Steve up (we were on a first-name basis now since we were going to dinner) at his hotel, and we drove to a favorite restaurant of ours in downtown Dayton. I knew it would be quiet and we could talk freely without prying ears nearby. We spent the first thirty minutes talking about family and our respective work lives. Finally, we got to the heart of the matter. While he couldn't offer me the job that night, he could start the process by referring me to Health and Human Services (HHS) personnel who handle such hires as well as the White House personnel that approve high-profile positions. We talked some more on the way back to his hotel as I kept asking all kinds of stupid questions about working for the federal government and having a $9 billion annual budget. We shook hands two and half hours after I picked him up, and I drove home in silence, deep in thought.

The next several weeks were spent writing my CV (which I had not done in the last thirty years), filling out forms, and talking to different people at HHS. All seemed to be going well, and I kept thinking that I'd have to make an actual decision whether to take the job or not soon. I even started looking online at apartments in DC and also seeing what they pay the Director of Head Start (it looked like $200,000). It was then I received an email to set up a call with the White House Personnel Office. It was scheduled quickly, and I began to prepare to talk about Head Start and my thoughts on its effectiveness and future direction. I did a fair amount of research and made some calls to folks I knew who were intimately familiar with the program.

When the time came for the call, I was more than prepared. With notes all around me, we started the call. There were two people on the other side, and they were polite and courteous but very direct and to the point. Not even a "How are you?" or "Thanks for taking the time." It was scheduled for thirty minutes, and we got right to it. It became clear immediately that my research and notes were useless. The questions were pretty simple. "Are you now or have you ever been associated with a 'Never Trump' group or movement?" This was followed by questions about guns and abortion and a few other conservative stalwart inquiries. It was over in about fifteen minutes without a single mention of early childhood or what I'd do with $9 billion.

I waited for a month before I reached out to anyone to check on the status of my application and the Head Start job. No one who answered the phone or replied to an email knew anything. Even the people who were responsive before went crickets on me. And nothing from Wagner. Finally, the friend at the think tank that started this ball rolling emailed me with news, but said it needed to be a call. Apparently, no trail was recommended for this communication. I called and was told I would not be offered the position due to two issues: I wasn't black, and I wasn't a woman. True and true. I said, "Well, I can't change one of those, and I won't change the other."

In looking back on it, it makes some sense and is typical of the sensitivity of appearances. We all wish that wasn't the case, but it is, especially with social services that serve women who are predominantly black. I wasn't too disappointed though. The job sounded entrenched in red tape and bureaucracy, and the program was not likely to change. It was, and still is, a lot like many other federal programs that start out with good intentions but have no accountability to outcomes or to the people they are supposed to serve. Some things are not likely to change.

For the next year, I stayed busy with my company and still made several trips to DC to advocate for early childhood issues. I continued to deliver speeches and make presentations across the country as well, and I probably have some small name for myself in this area. In November 2018, I received an invitation to join the National Board of Education Sciences. This is a body that makes decisions on research done by the Department of Education. Members of the board are appointed by the president of the United States by and with the consent of the Senate. I was already thinking *This will not go well,* but it was a different position than Head Start.

My conversations with the director of the Institution of Education Sciences at the Department of Education were great. We had a lot in common as far as philosophy on education and particularly the focus on the early years of children's lives. He seemed to genuinely look forward to working with me and said he would get the ball rolling with the approval process. I was glad he was confident, or at least not concerned, because the whole presidential appointment and Senate confirmation thing seemed like a big deal.

I was sent another set of forms to fill out. This time there were large bold letters at the bottom: "**INTERNAL WHITE HOUSE DOCUMENT, NOT FOR RELEASE WITHOUT PRIOR WHITE HOUSE APPROVAL.**" I'm probably in big trouble just writing that. The information they asked for was fairly straightforward background stuff. It was clear that there was a bent toward political leanings and published or public comments. I got it all completed and waited.

This time was not much different than Head Start. I didn't hear anything, and when I reached out to folks, they either didn't know or didn't answer again. Finally, I heard back from a source in the government with news, as long as I didn't repeat it or quote them. The answer was the same again—I would not be offered a seat on this board. This time the reason was different. There was only one reason this time, and I couldn't change this one either. The White House had apparently discovered the article by the reporter about my child support payments written during the election. It was enough to sink me.

I complained to the person about that article, how it was reck-lessly written and presented or implied things that were not true. I vented for a while even though I knew it wouldn't make a dif-ference. It just pissed me off all over again; like so many wrongs on the internet, you can't do a damn thing about their continued existence. Although I was obviously upset about the reason, I did have to laugh about President Trump letting "fake news" sway a decision. Thanks again to that reporter and her newspaper. The gift that keeps on giving.

Just when I thought I was permanently on the outs with this White House, I received an email invitation out of the blue. And it was directly from the White House. Seriously. Here it is:

> *Good Evening,*
>
> *We look forward to hosting you at the White House Summit on Child Care and Paid Leave, this **Thursday, December 12th at 9:00 a.m.** Please read this email in full as it pertains to important information regarding your visit.*
>
> ***LOCATION:** Eisenhower Executive Office Building (EEOB) on the White House Complex. South Court Auditorium.*
>
> ***ARRIVE AT:** 17th Street NW and State Place NW, Washington D.C., 20502. Attendees can begin arriving at 8:00 a.m. You will not be permitted to enter any earlier than this time.*
>
> *Upon your arrival, Secret Service will check your driver's license, passport, or other government-issued photo ID. This must be a current, valid form of identification. Paper copies and expired IDs will not be accepted. Keep in mind that if there are any discrepancies (including minor "typos") between the personal information that you submit and what is listed on your identifi-cation, this will delay your entrance into the EEOB. We strongly*

advise that all guests confirm that their personal information is correct before passing it along. If you experience issues at the gate, please contact Grace Skogman at 202-456-7696.

After your identification has been checked, you will go through security similar to what you are used to seeing at the airport. You will then be issued a temporary badge that will give you access to the Eisenhower Executive Office Building. Please plan to spend at least fifteen minutes passing through security.

***ITEMS ALLOWED**: Most items are allowed into the Eisenhower Executive Office Building. You'll be able to bring purses, backpacks, phones, luggage, etc. Prohibited items include guns, ammunition, fireworks, electric stun guns, mace, martial arts weapons/devices, or knives of any size. If you are unsure about a certain item, please feel free to reach out to our office for clarification.*

***FOOD/BEVERAGE**: Food is not provided at the conference. However, there is a cafeteria (Ike's) in the EEOB where items are available for purchase.*

***ATTIRE:** Business.*

Please let us know if you have any questions or concerns and we look forward to hosting you!

—The White House Office of Public Liaison

Honestly, my first thought was *This must be a joke.* The sender was "White House" and the email address was a "who.eop.gov". It looked legitimate as "who" is "White House Office," "eop" is "Executive Office of the President," and then ".gov." Still unsure, I looked for such an event online and found nothing. Then, I sent an email to my two senators' offices and asked for verification. Both responded and said it looked legit, but they didn't know anything else. Finally,

I talked to the folks at Council for a Strong America, a nonprofit where I am a board member and they verified it, as they had been asked to supply a few panelists for a discussion at the event.

I ended up going to the event and enjoying it. It was mostly a public relations event that showcased progress made by the administration on several issues. It was hosted by Ivanka Trump, and the president made an appearance and a few remarks. There were about a dozen members of the House and Senate there, along with several cabinet members. I met many of them and shook hands with Ivanka. The room held two hundred or so people, so I felt honored to be there although still unsure why I got invited. Maybe I somehow had rehabbed my "terrible" reputation.

On the Issues:
The Good, the Bad,
and the Need for Change

MY TIME SPENT RUNNING FOR Congress opened my eyes in a lot of ways. I learned about the nuts and bolts of campaigns. But I also learned about factors that are beyond a candidate's knowledge of issues—and potential ability to get things done—that determine the likelihood of winning an election. As I pointed out earlier, money is the biggest contributor, but there are other factors in the structure of elections that should be addressed to reduce money's influence and also improve the chances that we send qualified people to serve in Congress.

As I looked back on my own experience, I began to research ways to improve American elections. I was most interested in ideas that make it easier for candidates to be heard. These ideas weren't necessarily radical—they were simply improvements on existing processes. While the world has changed greatly since our Founding Fathers, our election system has not evolved in the best ways possible. I think we can get back to the ideals of electing great public servants.

What follows are my recommendations for reforms that will give voters a greater voice, while simultaneously reducing the influence of parties and outside money. If voters feel they really have a choice, and that they are not limited to the Republican or Democratic candidates, I believe more people would turn out and elections would be more reflective of voters' wishes.

In sum, campaigns should be simpler and more transparent, with reduced influence from campaign contributions and political parties—all of which will encourage candidates to speak their minds and appeal to a wider audience. And if we want more people to vote, we should expand opportunities for voting.

Campaign Finance

PACs: PACs, Super PACs, 501(c)(4)s, and the Supreme Court's *Citizens United v. FEC* decision have turned the financing of campaigns and candidates into a messy storm of disinformation that most voters cannot figure out. It doesn't have to be that way, but the solutions are a bit messy too.

For most Americans, the distinction between a PAC, Super PAC, and 501(c)(4) is a blur, if they know what any of them are to begin with. And *Citizens United* may remind them of a lawsuit or U.S. Supreme Court ruling, or could even be synonymous with big money influence in elections. I don't think any of this is too complicated if boiled down to simple terms, and the differences are important. What follows is a boiling down, with the caveat that there are details to each that matter but can be forgone for now.

PAC is short for "political action committee." PACs have existed since 1944, and they raise and spend money to elect and/or defeat candidates. Most PACs are formed to represent a particular interest, whether it be issue(s), candidate(s), or more broadly the interests of its funders. Think of it as typically being used for a certain industry, a single company, unions, or an issue like abortion or guns.

PACs can give a maximum of $5,000 per candidate per election (primary and general are each one election), $5,000 annually to other PACs, and $15,000 annually to a national party (Republican, Democrat, etc.). They can receive an annual maximum of $5,000 from any one person or entity.

Super PACs: Super PACs started being created in 2010, following a U.S. Court of Appeals ruling, *SpeechNow.org v. Federal Elections Commission*, which extended First Amendment rights from individuals to groups of people who pool their money to speak on an issue or a candidate. Just like it is everyone's individual right to speak without limit about a candidate, the court ruled it is the same for a group. To ban or limit a group's right to speak was deemed a violation of the First Amendment, so the Super PAC was born.

These PACs make no contributions to candidates or parties but spend money independently on federal races, much like a candidate's campaign would. The big difference with a Super PAC is that the donations and expenditures are unlimited (but must be from within the United States), and they are not allowed to coordinate (talk or plan how to spend money) with a candidate's campaign.

Both PACs and Super PACs are required to file with the Federal Elections Commission (FEC) and list their donations by donor and expenditures. The donations are not tax deductible, just like contributions to a campaign are not.

All of this may seem like Super PACs don't sound so bad, but there is a major distinction. They are allowed to accept money from incorporated entities that do not have to make the sources of their funding public. This means the actual donors remain undisclosed and hidden from public scrutiny.

Super PAC example: The Club for Growth is a multifaceted organization (with PAC and Super PAC) whose main mission since its founding in 1999 has been to get ultra-conservative candidates elected to Congress. They have been so hell-bent on this mission that their targets were more often fellow Republicans than Democrats. The Club quickly became popular among Tea Party members and other fiscal hawks and a thorn in the side of any sitting member of Congress who ever had a single centrist thought.

Traditionally funded by a handful of extremely wealthy white men, their influence grew, and the members of Congress they helped get elected became louder. Their voices organized within Congress through the House Freedom Caucus and contributed to John Boehner's resignation as well as a splintering of the House Republicans, including the party's ability to message as a unified body.

The Club's ability to influence Republican races was unparalleled for over a decade. Their peak was likely just as I was running for office. Interestingly, since then it seems to have waned. It could be that their early and strong opposition to Trump infamously backfired on them or that many Republicans and their backers are tired of the endless civil war inside the Republican Party that Club started and continues to ferment. It's doubtful that Club will go away, but their influence and effectiveness is not the same today as it was in 2016.

501(c)(4): A 501(c)(4) is so-called because that is the section of IRS code that defines it. Two types of organizations are allowed by this section. The political one is for "social welfare" organizations and must operate to promote just that—social welfare. These organizations can lobby for issues and legislative change. They cannot participate in candidate campaigns. Like PACs and Super PACs, donations are not tax deductible. However, unlike PACs and Super PACs, donors and expenditures are not subject to FEC rules and are not public.

Citizens United*: Citizens United* is short for a lawsuit brought by a group named Citizens United against the IRS. The U.S. Supreme Court ruled that it was legal for corporations and other outside groups to spend unlimited money on elections. The decision was based on the First Amendment, which guarantees the right to free speech.

This decision dramatically increased spending on elections by wealthy individuals, corporations, and special interest groups. It also ushered in a new wave of Super PACs that allowed donors to obscure the origination of their funding. The only restriction left by the decision was that these organizations could not coordinate with campaigns.

The impact of *Citizens United* has been huge. In the last ten years, Super PACs have spent over $3 billion on federal elections. Most Senate races see significant outside spending from Super PACs on the winning candidate. It is also possible, due to the lack of transparency as to their donors, that foreign individuals, corporations, or even governments may be funders.

Overall, 501(c)(4)s pose the same problem as Super PACs with their lack of transparency and ability to hide the source of their funding.

Summary

In more practical terms, what does all this mean? First, PACs will exist and contribute to campaigns, although their amounts will be modest. Remember the $5,000 per candidate per election rule. Second, Super PACs can be big influencers. They potentially have unlimited resources and could easily swing an election. (The average amount of money spent by the winner of a U.S. House of Representatives seat was $1.5 million in 2016.)[18] Third, you will sometimes see a 501(c)(4) play in the political arena by way of indirectly advocating for a candidate. They do this by publicly advocating for candidates who support their social welfare issue. You often see this as a "rank and shame" showing who supports an issue and who doesn't.

Solutions

While there is not an easy set of solutions to these issues, we should all be concerned about the flow of large amounts of money into federal elections without any traceability. Here are a few suggestions for reform.

1. We should hope for a reversal of *Citizens United*. This is unlikely, due to the U.S. Supreme Court's reluctance to overturn their earlier decisions, but Congress can diminish the impact of *Citizens United* impact through new laws requiring greater transparency on donations above a certain amount ($2,000) and overall caps ($2,000–4,000).

2. We should expand public funding of campaigns. This is unlikely and probably unpopular, but options include offering a public match (6:1) of small donations ($200 or less) paid for

by surcharges or levies on campaign violations. Some examples of these types of reforms can already be found in Oregon, Maryland, and Alaska where they work and are paid for.

3. We should advocate for stronger disclosure and transparency in election spending. Some of this could come from the FEC improving and updating its rules. This is possible, but don't hold your breath.

4. We should fix the FEC. It starts by electing lawmakers that will pass legislation to overcome its shortcomings. Specifically, (1) we should pass a complete reform of campaign finance laws, of which the centerpiece is fixing the inherent problems of oversight within the FEC. An imperfect bill known as the "For The People Act" contains several such actions. A more detailed set of recommendations is available from the Brennan Center for Justice in an article by Daniel Weiner titled "Fixing the FEC: An Agenda for Reform."[19] In essence, the FEC has not updated it rules nor provided anywhere near adequate oversight for the past decade. Most of this is a structural problem and not difficult to solve.

Making elections fair and transparent is what all of us—or at least the vast majority of us—want. No matter what party you are in or what values you lean toward, Americans just want to know elections are conducted with all the rigor you expect from one of our most foundational rights, the right to elect our representatives. We also want to know who's paying for campaign expenditures and anything remotely tied to influencing our votes. We won't stop the influence of outside money with the power of knowledge. Let's press hard for Congress to reform campaign finance and restore the FEC to its original intent, guarding the integrity of our elections.

Three more ideas for reform

1. Abolish publicly financed primaries.
2. Enact state laws that require safe and secure procedures for the use of mail-in ballots and provide every registered voter with such a ballot. Better yet, do the same for electronic voting systems.
3. Enact ranked-choice voting (RCV).

Primaries

There are three fundamental reasons to eliminate primaries.

1. They are ridiculously expensive for the taxpayers and create no apparent added value. While the precise cost of primaries is difficult to estimate (states oversee elections, but individual counties run them), a few studies have concluded that it likely is $500 million or more per election.[20] This does not include run-offs that occur in certain states due to an inability to get to a threshold of votes by any one candidate.
2. There is low turnout among primary voters.
3. Only the candidates representing the two major parties emerge as victors in the primaries, and they are being chosen by a small subset of voters. One of the candidates is often the incumbent, who has significant fundraising advantages and strong name recognition. The other party's winner is often a dead man walking in the usual gerrymandered district. Both tend to be candidates pandering to the further right or further left of their respective parties. And typically, neither candidate possesses much appeal to members of the other party.

The parties should be free to do whatever they want, such as holding and financing their own endorsement events. But give the rest of us a chance to consider a wider array of choices that aren't always playing to the extremes.

Mail-In and Future Electronic Balloting

COVID-19 showed us what the future of voting could look like. There will be more choices in the future, and we should embrace them just as we have embraced other new facets of dealing with security-sensitive changes in our lives. And, yes, security and protection from fraud are required for their success.

In the future, it will be possible to do just about everything online, short of actions such as flying somewhere on an airplane. But other activities you *don't* have to do in person—like paying your taxes, paying your bills, renewing car and driver licenses (no longer required in person in Ohio), investing money, renewing a passport, or even renewing my Global Entry membership through U.S. Customs and Border Protection (this is an expedited screening for international travel—kind of like the TSA Pre-Check)—will be available online (and maybe exclusively online). If the federal government including the IRS and U.S. Customs and the state of Ohio allow me to do important and critical actions online, then voting can be done securely by mail and eventually by electronic means in the near future.

Ranked-Choice Voting (RCV)

I see this as the foundation of election reform, with its enactment leading to higher-quality elected officials. Suspend your "one person—one vote" mindset for a few minutes and let me explain.

Let's take a general election for a single office, say the U.S. Congress seat of your home district. The way we vote now is that each person has *one vote*. You go into the voting booth (or get online someday!) and cast that one, single vote for one, single person. The ballot may have two or ten people on the list but you get one vote. When balloting closes, the votes are tallied, and your state tabulates who won. Most states will award the election to who has the most votes although there are caveats that may require run-offs or recounts.

With RCV, the ballot looks like this:

PREFERENCE RANKING

	1st Choice	2nd Choice	3rd Choice	4th Choice
Candidate A	●	○	○	○
Candidate B	○	○	○	●
Candidate C	○	○	●	○
Candidate D	○	●	○	○

Instead of casting one vote for one candidate, you get to rank each candidate in order of preference. You can rank only one, rank them all, or anything in between. Your choice.

In the current system, a winner is declared when a candidate receives over 50 percent of the votes. So what happens when no one receives over 50 percent of the votes? With one vote per person, the candidate with the most votes usually wins. But wait, that means someone with far less than 50 percent could win, right? Someone with less than 33 percent, which means two times as many people voted against this candidate as voted for them! Or, in some states, it may mean an expensive and time-consuming run-off election held at a later date. This means more tax dollars spent and a delay in preparing for office.

When this happens with RCV, the process is simple. The candidate receiving the least number of first-place votes is eliminated and those who have this candidate ranked as their first choice then have their second choice counted. Here's a graphic showing this:

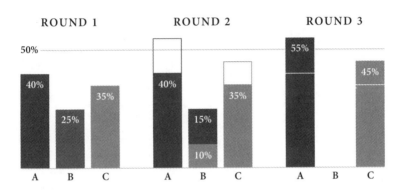

Some may say this is confusing, but it is just that simple. If you voted for, say, the third-place candidate, the tallying goes on and your vote, and your voice, still count. Who would want their opinion on a federal election discarded just because their first choice wound up last? Of course, you'd still want to be heard.

Consider an everyday example of this, because I guarantee you use RCV every day in your life and almost never, if ever, use one vote per person.

In my personal life, many days a week are concluded with an all-important topic: "Where are we going for dinner?" Sometimes, it's just my wife and I, and then she wins because I am a smart husband. Other times, we may have some of our kids at home and maybe an in-law. Then the conversation starts, and guess what? It's never one vote/one person. It's a discussion that resembles RCV and its tallying procedure. It's quick (well, sometimes) and easy. Take a look at this:

A Family at Dinnertime			
Where do you want to eat?			
	1ST CHOICE	**2ND CHOICE**	**3RD CHOICE**
Dad	**The Capital Grille**	Ruth's Chris	Firebirds
Mom	**The Capital Grille**	Ruth's Chris	Firebirds
25-year-old son	Noodles & Co.	**The Capital Grille**	B.J.'s
17-year-old son	Marion's Piazza	**The Capital Grille**	Fricker's
15-year-old son	McDonald's	Skyline Chili	Gold Star Chili
12-year-old daughter	McDonald's	Wendy's	Taco Bell
8-year-old daughter	McDonald's	Taco Bell	Chucky Cheese
Mother-in-law	Noodles & Co.	**The Capital Grille**	Redlands
TALLY	**ROUND 1**	**ROUND 2**	**ROUND 3**
McDonald's	3	3	3
The Capital Grille	2	3	5
Noodles & Co.	2	2	Out
Marion's Piazza	1	Out	
If one vote, then we're eating at McDonald's. Ugh!			
If RCV, then it's the Capital Grille. Steak, baby!			

Dad and Mom like good food from good restaurants. Some of the kids have little to no palate. Look at the first round. If we're counting as one vote/one person, then they are eating Big Macs and the adults aren't happy because they "split the vote," so to speak. McDonald's got the most and, in this case, 38 percent. In my house, after the first vote, there is hemming and hawing around and discussing, maybe even a little negotiating, but in the end, it looks like RCV. In the example, Marion's Piazza is eliminated after the first round and the seventeen-year-old's vote goes to The Capital Grille. But since there is still not a majority agreement, it goes to the second round of tallying and Noodles & Co. is eliminated. That means twenty-five-year-old son and mom-in-law go to their second choice, which is The Capital Grille. Now, The Capital Grille has 63 percent and wins. Note that the third choice was never used for anyone but shown as an example.

I intentionally made this seem complicated, but think of how this actually works at your house. It is the same. Everyone's vote counts until there is a majority. Otherwise, the minority rebels or feels unvalued, like their vote didn't count or was wasted.

Let me offer a simpler example: In most businesses (including mine), no major decision, in fact, no decision of any type, is ever made using one vote/one person. Why? In business, this type of decision-making would be the opposite of building consensus, valuing opinions, and making sure everyone was heard and accounted for. At the highest levels in corporations, it is the same. In board rooms across the country, every day major decisions get made using an RCV philosophy, if not actual procedure.

Look at the following table illustrating a meeting of directors at a hypothetical company. They meet annually and make decisions about how much money to spend investing in the growth of their business. The three options are laid out by the CEO and his team. They vary quite a bit and will have large ramifications on their future. Underinvesting could cause them to miss a market upturn that they will not be able to regain. Overinvesting runs the risk of financial ruin by purchasing capital equipment that sits idle. Their choice in capital spending is either aggressive, moderate, or conservative. Here is what RCV looks like in this case:

A Company's Board of Directors		
What's the strategic plan for next year?		
DIRECTOR #	1ST CHOICE	2ND CHOICE
1	Aggressive	Moderate
2	Aggressive	Moderate
3	Aggressive	Moderate
4	Aggressive	Moderate
5	Moderate	Conservative
6	Moderate	Conservative
7	Moderate	Conservative
8	Conservative	Moderate
9	Conservative	Moderate
	44% Aggressive	56% Moderate
	33% Moderate	44% Aggressive
	22% Conservative	0% Conservative
If one vote, then with a tally of 4-3-2, they choose Aggressive.		
If RCV, then it's 5-4 and they're playing it Moderate.		

Note here that if the company took one vote/one person to heart, it would have wound up with an aggressive strategy. However, it took only one extra round after the initial vote to establish that the moderate strategy won out.

Look closer and think about what would have happened in that boardroom. The initial discussion would have shown opinions across the entire spectrum, but a discussion would have led to both conservative and aggressive being in the moderate column and the decision likely would have been unanimous. With RCV as an example process, the answer was the same.

RCV is not new nor radical nor untried. It is currently used in more than twenty-six U.S. cities across fourteen states and in two states for statewide elections.[21] It is also used in many universities and organizations. In 2020, Maine used RCV for its presidential general election. Australia (the country with the highest voter turnout in the world), New Zealand, and Ireland use it for national elections.

My point is obvious. We all use a form of RCV every day in our lives. We don't use one vote/one person. To roll all of this together, wouldn't we all like to see elections financed with true transparency, limited dark money involvement, an FEC that does its job, no primaries so we can all vote on all the candidates at the same time, and a system that rewards less negativity and more choice without runoffs? Let's get our public officials to wake up and bring our election system into the twenty-first century. We deserve it as Americans, and our country needs it to prosper.

Gerrymandering

Gerrymandering is a big and insidious problem. States are unlikely to resolve it, so minimizing its impact is paramount. Let's look at it in practical terms.

Gerrymandering is the practice of drawing congressional districts so that they favor one party over the other. Most people have heard of it, but not everyone appreciates the full effects it can have on elections and representation. A better definition might be manipulating the boundaries of a district so profoundly that they make no sense to anyone who looks at it. Want an example that drives this home? Take a look at the following graphics.[22]

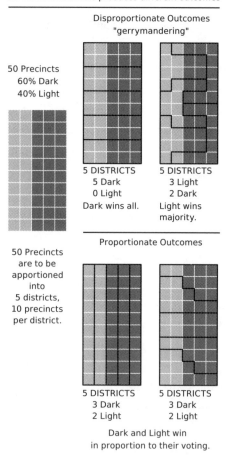

Gerrymandering: drawing different maps
for electoral districts produces different outcomes

Disproportionate Outcomes
"gerrymandering"

50 Precincts
60% Dark
40% Light

50 Precincts
are to be
apportioned
into
5 districts,
10 precincts
per district.

5 DISTRICTS
5 Dark
0 Light
Dark wins all.

5 DISTRICTS
3 Light
2 Dark
Light wins
majority.

Proportionate Outcomes

5 DISTRICTS
3 Dark
2 Light

5 DISTRICTS
3 Dark
2 Light

Dark and Light win
in proportion to their voting.

Of the four possible district drawings, take a close look at the upper left. It is drawn so that *every* district is darkly shaded. That is the very essence of gerrymandering.

If you are tempted to ask, "So what?" or argue that the lines are drawn fairly since Dark has the majority, consider that both Democrats and Republicans have been guilty of this, so hypothetically you could be a Light voter someday. We all want to be fairly represented and not gerrymandered out of that right.

The history of gerrymandering is fairly straightforward. Initially, each House member was to represent about 30,000 people. It was set to that size with the philosophy that each representative could get to know their constituents and represent them well. Consistent with that philosophy, the number of members in the House increased every decade. But in 1910, the number of House members was capped at 435, which is where it remains today. After each census, the 435 are reapportioned to the states based on their population, and the district maps are redrawn accordingly. (A side note: at the rate of one representative per 30,000 people, there would be 11,000 members of the House!)

Some have argued that we need more representatives and have even devised mathematical equations to make this work. An example is to have the number of representatives be the cube root of the population, which would mean 691 members. (Some other countries do something like this.) Under this proposal, the House would have between 600 and 700 members. I think this might be a good idea, but it would not address gerrymandering, so it's a side issue to me.

There are countless examples of gerrymandering, since each state decides on their own how to draw district lines. The only federal law requirements are that they must be of equal size and not discriminate on the basis of race or ethnicity. States decide everything else on their own.

How well has this worked? In Ohio, not so well. The following map shows Ohio's Eighth Congressional District in 2016 when I ran. It had been drawn by Republicans when Boehner was Speaker, and he undoubtedly influenced it so that his reelections were easy. Also, the lines were drawn so that the districts of Boehner and another representative touched or were adjacent to Wright Patterson Air Force Base, a very important Department of Defense installation that employs 28,000 people on one site.

Then, in 2018, Ohio voters got fed up with the state's district-drawing shenanigans. Nearly 75 percent of them supported a referendum, known as Issue 1, which amended Ohio's constitution to bring greater bipartisanship and transparency to the redistricting process. Good intentions aside, the amendment didn't fix the process fully and instead has resulted in one that has frustrated both Republicans and Democrats.

It actually created a ridiculously complex system. Essentially, the legislature can impose a new map if 60 percent of the legislators support it, including half the minority. That never happens (anywhere). Upon this failure, a commission of seven elected officials, including the governor and four others from his party, but only two Democrats, can draw the map. If they fail (and they do), then it's back to the legislature, where members can pass a map if one-third of the minority supports it. If that doesn't work (and it never does), then eventually the majority party can draw the district lines without any support from the minority, but in that case, the district lines only stand for four years instead of ten. Got it?

In 2022, as this book was going to press, a new congressional map for Ohio had been drawn and approved, but Ohio's Supreme Court had rejected the fourth attempt to redraw state representative and senate district lines. As a result, the initial primary date for those elections was canceled and not rescheduled due to the uncertainty.

Ohio is not the only state that struggles with gerrymander-minded malaise. Take a look at the districts below from two other states. Without any explanation or narrative, you can tell how crazy this has become.

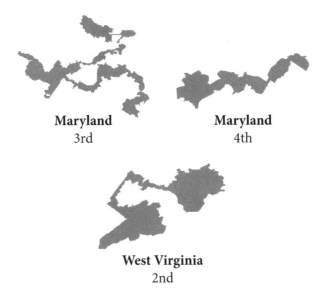

Maryland
3rd

Maryland
4th

West Virginia
2nd

So what's the solution? Many have said "independent" commissions. This makes sense on the surface, but the devil is in the details. Developing a system that creates a truly independent commission is probably almost impossible. It is a worthy goal but not realistic.

I would advocate for a design that removes the human component and creates districts that are as compact as possible. Splitting cities or neighborhoods in suburban areas makes no sense at all. Algorithms have been created that simulate this and could be refined to take the people and politics out of the equation.

Voter Turnout

Voter turnout is terrible in primaries and limits the quality and type of candidates we get from both parties, thereby diminishing the quality and popularity of elected officials.

We would all like to think more people should vote. And when they vote, we also hope they go into the ballot booth, or sit at the kitchen table with their ballot, and are informed. The history of voter turnout is consistent in some ways and varies a lot in other ways. What follows is what we know about voter turnout in presidential elections since 1980. (I've excluded off-years because that will only depress you, as they are significantly worse.):[23]

However you measure it, voter turnout jumped in 2020

Votes cast in U.S. presidential race as % of indicated population

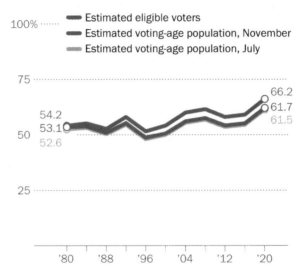

This looks promising, although it is clear that the turnout increase for 2020 was mostly due to more broadly used mail-in ballots (almost half the total) and possibly some sort of "Trump Effect," whether positively or negatively viewed as such. This could all be good news if the trend continues, as it likely will.

Now let's look at primaries from 1980 to 2016. The chart on the next page shows what that looks like:[24]

After a long decline, primary turnout rebounds

Votes cast in Democratic and Republican primaries as a share of eligible voters in primary states

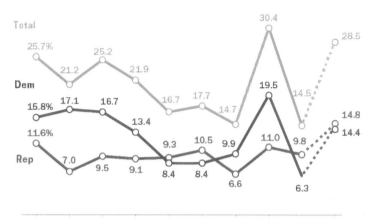

It's a bit choppier and doesn't match up so well with the first chart. Notice in the first chart that there was not a spike in 2008, and the increase in 2016 was not as sharp. So, what happened in 2020, you ask?

Here are some numbers of interest from the 2020 primaries:[25]

Average		24%
Low		3% (ND)
High		46% (MT)
Early States:	IA	9%
	NH	42%
	NV	5% (Democrat only)
	SC	14% (Democrat only)

Biggest States:	CA	38%
	TX	21%
	FL	20%
	NY	6%
	PA	28%
	IL	25%
	OH	21%
Average		*23% (below the national average)*

I laid out more detail for 2020 to show the granular data but also to highlight that there is a lot of variation in the state numbers that the national numbers don't capture. When broken down into parties, we see that only 21.6 million Republicans voted, versus 36.5 million Democrats, although a portion of this is explained by the incumbent president being a Republican.

Compared to the rest of the developed countries in the world, the United States lags behind quite a bit. According to the Organization of Economic Cooperation and Development, we are ranked 30 out of the top 35 developed countries in eligible voters who are registered, and we lag behind in percent of registered voters who actually vote. Australia is the leader in registered voters who vote: 92 percent.[26]

The takeaway is that a small percentage of voters are deciding who will be on the ballot each November. These small groups of primary voters often represent the extremes, or at least further edges, of each party. It is often the far-right and far-left candidates battling each other in the general elections, causing most of us to vote with our noses held tightly.

Just as with gerrymandering, there is not much to do here to solve this problem. We all wish more people would vote and that those who do vote would be well informed. Let's keep wishing for that, but in the meantime, instituting RCV and eliminating primaries are some possible avenues for improvement.

Improving Congress

I have a few thoughts on how Congress might be made to function closer to how our Founding Fathers envisioned it and how I believe we all would like to see it today.

The Founding Fathers laid out our government in the U.S. Constitution. One of their primary concerns at the time was balancing power between the executive, legislative, and judiciary branches of government. James Madison was particularly sensitive to tensions between the president and Congress. He wanted to keep that powerful human constant, ambition, in check between political branches.

Today, tension between the two political parties exceeds tension between the branches of government. Many, if not most, members of the House are willing to subordinate their interests, independence, and good judgment to their party leaders. And for the party holding the presidency, House members of the same party will typically subordinate their interests to those of the president. The result has been the highest degree of dysfunction. The party in power is simply interested in jamming its agenda through, by whatever means necessary, while the minority only strategizes how to stop them. Legislating, or discussing issues and finding common ground, is all but dead.

Restoring effective and productive governing in Congress will be difficult but not impossible. Here are a few ideas.

House of Representatives

The House of Representatives is a mess. While it was meant to be the body that produces most of our legislation, it has turned into a place where only the majority's bills see the light of day, and breaking with one's party can bring all sorts of unpleasant repercussions. For the minority party, the focus is often just being an attack dog. It's hard to completely blame the minority (whichever party that is) given there is no chance to be heard, but it is frustrating that the tone is so rancorous.

What could be done? The procedural rules and ways of the House need to change. Some of the changes could actually be modest:

1. Prohibit fundraising on days when the House is in session.
2. Enforce the three-day rule for legislation to be read and considered before votes (this rule is frequently suspended).
3. Add time for debate.
4. Require minimum co-sponsor thresholds of 60 percent to move legislation forward.

The biggest change, and thus the most difficult to implement, would be to curtail the power of the elected party leaders and redirect that power to the committees.

The diminished power and influence of committee chairs has been evident for several decades. The result has been less and less productive work emanating from the committees. This is disconcerting, given that it's the committees that have traditionally informed legislation and guided bipartisan work. Such work is almost nonexistent now, as legislative agendas are set often without input from these committees and prior to them meeting. Much committee work has now devolved into hearings where congressmen pontificate and grab as many headlines as possible. The work of the committees needs to be restored, but the agenda and power of the committee leadership needs balancing, just as does the House and Senate leadership.

The parliamentarian in both the House and the Senate—each body has one—can play a critical role in improving the effectiveness of both institutions. A nonpartisan, unelected position, the parliamentarian is the authoritative voice on each chamber's rules, with a high level of deference given to their rulings and advice on interpretation of the rules and how to apply them. Not since 1975 has a majority leader overruled the parliamentarian.

The parliamentarian (or their staff member on duty while in session) also interprets other unwritten rules and precedents. While not official rules, these are nonetheless just as important, given that there are substantial written understandings of how these other rules and precedents work. For example, one of the most famous ones is the so-called Byrd Rule. It states the Senate is "prohibited from considering extraneous matter as part of a reconciliation bill or resolution or conference report thereon." It further defines an "extraneous matter."[27]

The parliamentarian is appointed by the majority leader of each chamber and serves at the pleasure of that leader. Change of parliamentarians does not occur often—the previous two served in the Senate for ten years. Whenever you hear the parliamentarian being mentioned in the news, it is often because there is a dispute about an interpretation of a rule or precedent. Sometimes it may be a bit wonky to listen to, but other times it may signal that one side or the other is trying to bend or break a rule. I always perk up when I hear them mentioned.

The Senate

There has been less institutional damage to the Senate than the House, and it remains the more deliberative body of the two. It is much rarer to see a fellow senator treat another without respect and cordiality. However, the Senate could use the same leadership changes as the House. It could also stand to restore some of the rules that have made it a hallmark of even and considered legislating. The filibuster is one such rule. While much maligned, it is the perfect example of a rule that promotes writing and passing great legislation.

Both Democrats and Republicans will incessantly blame the other for relying on the filibuster to delay legislation or nominations, while the public decries the fact that our government doesn't function. In these polarizing political times, it is legitimate to think there must be a better way. It makes more sense to me to briefly review what a filibuster is and why it is useful to keep as part of the Senate rules.

The Senate is governed by forty-four standing rules. Most of them are pretty mundane. Things like when they come to work, the order they talk about things, how to vote, committee formations and how they're run, and several rules that make it clear what you can't do with money. The filibuster is part of Rule 22 (or XXII to be precise), which is titled "Precedence of Motions." This rule ensures that there's a big difference between how the Senate works and how the House of Representatives works, where simple majorities are all it takes to pass most everything. In the most recently published version of these rules, Rule 22 takes up only about two pages. It is simple and straightforward, even though it causes more consternation than the other forty-three rules put together.

First, a brief (I promise) history. "Filibuster" is the term used to describe taking advantage of the Senate's tradition of allowing unlimited debate on an issue to delay a vote. It has been used since the birth of our country. Until recently, a filibuster required senators to be present and speak on the floor. Senator Strom Thurmond famously (infamously?) holds the record of speaking for more than twenty-four consecutive hours. The longest continuous filibuster, involving multiple senators, came during the debate over the Civil Rights Act of 1964, and it lasted for sixty days.[28] Today, senators are not required to actually speak in the chamber. They simply tell Senate leadership that they intend to filibuster and go back to their office.

Filibusters can end one of two ways. Either when the speakers stop speaking or, today, when they tell leadership they are done with the filibuster. This usually because they have negotiated an acceptable change. Or, through invoking "cloture," which is a vote to end debate (the filibuster). Starting in 1917, this required a two-thirds majority. In 1975, this was amended to three-fifths. There are exceptions in the case of presidential nominees, including judicial appointments. The number of votes taken to end debate never reached one hundred in any two-year session of Congress until 2007-2008. It reached a record of 298 in the 2019-2020 Congress.

The filibuster is absolutely useful and should be maintained. Without the sixty-vote minimum to move forward on legislation, the Senate becomes just another version of the House and there-fore more likely to shift directions based on the current majority, which can change every two years due to the terms of every House member. These quick alterations in legislating from the House also change due to vagaries of the press and public perception. Even the current Democratic leader of the Senate, Chuck Schumer, who has been known to threaten to kill the filibuster while he is in the majority, has said, "The legislative filibuster is the most important distinction between the Senate and the House. Without the sixty-vote threshold for legislation, the Senate becomes a majoritarian institution, just like the House, much more subject to the winds of short-term electoral change. No senator would like to see that happen." This was in April 2017, when he was in the minority.[29]

Many of the Senate's other rules require it to come to unanimous consent. This includes adjusting the hours it is in session, whether certain speeches can be made on the floor, whether legislative text needs to be read in its entirety, and many more mundane decisions. The unanimity means senators are expected to be in accord with each other to process the Senate's business. It requires all of them to take into account their own actions and how they affect every other senator. It promotes thoughtfulness, consensus, professionalism, and courtesy. Given that these attributes are largely absent in the House, I support preserving the Senate's rules so that the other half maintains the ideals that we would all like to see our legislators strive for every day.

The other positive part of the Senate rules and its most important one, Rule 22, is that it forces the body to be more deliberate and collaborative. Laws that may exist on our nation's books for decades and centuries deserve an abundance of care and caution. Without it, the majority may often be tempted to pass laws that will only be overturned when, in the future, they are inevitably in the minority. This whipsaw effect would cause our nation to always be in a state of flux. Stability and predictability are cornerstones of our country. While we change to reflect a changing nation and its needs to maintain security and prosperity, the winds of change should be approached cautiously and with adequate time for debate, and yes, compromise. This is what sustainable and productive change requires of its lawmakers.

Is Your Congressman Effective?

The answer to this question is in the eye of the beholder. But other than watching him or her on TV or reading articles of interviews where the congressman is controlling the narrative, how might we judge the effectiveness of a member of Congress?

I ran for Congress because I wanted to make a difference; to me, that meant doing the job of legislator to the best of my ability, by being well informed on the issues, sticking with facts and evidence, avoiding polarizing or highly partisan rhetoric, advocating for commonsense approaches to governing, and focusing on legislation that improves our country and the lives of its citizens.

The last part was the most important in my mind. It seemed that to be a "legislator," you focused on legislation. Legislation that is authored, sponsored, co-sponsored, voted into law, funded, and implemented effectively. And to do that, it meant showing up every day ready for work and doing your job. I don't find it much more complicated than that, and for those who say otherwise, I would say you're not doing your job.

If I'm right about the "job" described here, I would then look to sources that indicate whether a congressman is, in fact, doing his or her job. The voting record is among the first places to look for evidence. Obviously, that can tell you whether the member's votes align with your positions, and it can also tell if he or she voted at all or were absent for many such votes. It's surprising how some congressmen miss that simple job requirement of voting.

Another meaningful source for me has been the Center for Effective Lawmaking (CEL), which is housed at the University of Virginia (UVA) and staffed along with Vanderbilt University. UVA has long been known for its work in politics and making accurate forecasts of elections as well as appraisals of candidates' strength in coming elections. For each Congress, they tabulate results from fifteen measures and release scores for every congressman. They also produce an array of research on how policymakers are effective and what makes them so. You can find their work at thelawmakers.org.

In the most recent ratings from the 116th Congress (2019-2020), the CEL found coalition-building and reaching across the aisle to be a key ingredient for the most effective congressmen, minority status did not impede effectiveness, and that women continue to score well. Interestingly, the most effective representatives and senators are not always the best known or appear on your TV often. Could it be that working gets in the way of sound bites and vice versa?

Alexandria Ocasio-Cortez (AOC) gets lots of headlines. It's almost as if her voice is louder than almost all other Democrats in the House. But the CEL ranked her only the 230th most effective Democrat (out of 240). She introduced twenty-one bills, but none of them went anywhere, meaning even the committees didn't do anything with them and they never saw the light of day.

Jim Jordan, a Republican from my home state of Ohio, is on TV a lot. He is mostly complaining about Democrats. He had the third lowest effectiveness score among all House Republicans. He introduced *one* bill, and it went nowhere. Warren Davidson—who won the Republican primary in which I was a candidate—was not much better, ranking 150th of 205 Republicans. He introduced eleven bills that went nowhere.

For reference, the leading Republican House member was Michael McCaul from Texas. He introduced thirty-five bills and had eleven bills receive action in committee, twelve bills receive action beyond committee, eleven bills pass the House, and three become law.

Pretty impressive work, and I can't tell you if I've ever seen him on TV or in the newspaper. I guess he works hard and does his job!

For fans of AOC and/or Jordan, I will admit that I see "some" value to what they do. Advocating loudly and strongly for what you believe in is part of the job. When in the minority, as was Jordan in the 116th Congress, it might be argued that there was little legislating to do or have input on, and pointing out the shortcomings of the majority agenda was needed. I get it to a point, but not completely, given that his record of legislative effectiveness hasn't really changed whether in the majority or minority.

These ratings may not be everything for most people, and I don't think they should. But they offer important insight on what your congressman is doing and whether he or she deserves your continued support.

Other Issues

While the aforementioned reform suggestions have been focused on issues related to Congress, I can't help but weigh in on a few other topics.

U.S. Supreme Court

The basics of the Supreme Court have remained largely the same since the court was established by Article III of the U.S. Constitution. Since 1969, there have always been nine justices, all appointed by the president and approved by the Senate. Each is appointed for life, meaning they can serve as long as they want.

The courts are the third branch of the federal government, and they are thoroughly independent, as they should be. Supreme

Court justices rule on cases based on law. As current Chief Justice John Roberts said during his confirmation hearing, "Judges are like umpires. Umpires don't make the rules; they apply them. The role of an umpire and a judge is critical. They make sure everybody plays by the rules, but it is a limited role. Nobody ever went to a ball game to see the umpire."[30] That sums it up perfectly.

Despite some efforts in the past to increase the number of justices beyond the current level, it has never gained traction. The reason why seems obvious. When this issue gets raised, the chief complainer is always some group or faction not getting their way with Supreme Court rulings.

This is utter nonsense. If we were to allow this to happen, it would be never-ending. When one side gets to raise the number to overcome the current majority, it would only last until they inevitably are not in power and the other side would raise the number even higher. You can easily see this fool's game leading to a court with ninety-nine justices instead of the current nine. Let's leave this alone and stop talking about it.

The issues that may be worth addressing are some of the ones that have caused discomfort. Let's look at them.

Terms and Term Limits

Some have called for terms such as ten or twenty years and/or term limits. This flies in the face of independence and stability and should not be considered. Lifetime appointments virtually guarantee independence of this critical branch of our government.

Mandatory Retirement Age

This should be appealing to anyone with a parent who aged a bit beyond their prime. Maybe they aren't losing all their faculties, but it is hard to imagine someone in their nineties, as was Justice Oliver Wendell Holmes Jr., functioning as well as someone in their fifties or sixties. Today, we are living longer and in better health longer than ever before. Although it is common for justices today to serve into their eighties, I would suggest age seventy-five as a reasonable retirement age.

Nomination and Senate Approval

Although the Senate has written rules that are clearly defined, it also has a long history of following other rules not formally adopted but also written. This should be done with Supreme Court nominations. The disagreement on taking up a nomination only occurs when the Senate majority is of a different party than the president, and it is an election year. That's fine and even logical, but let's make a rule for these circumstances and follow it.

The rule could be based on what has at times been called the "Biden Rule." It holds that a nomination should not be considered when it is close to a presidential election, or some would say, in the year of a presidential election. Given that a typical Supreme Court calendar begins the first Monday in October each year and ends in June, I think a vacancy occurring in January through June would not get filled in time to affect decisions already in process. There are no sessions during the summer, so the earliest impact of a new justice would be starting in October.

The rule I would suggest is that the Senate need not take up a nomination in the calendar year of a presidential election.

This would never impact the court if the President and Senate were of the same party. It would rarely impact a case heard or ruled on through June. It would impact the cases heard from October through December. However, the reality is that even if a nomination was taken up, it likely would not pass during an election year unless a president nominated an unusual judge who was acceptable to both sides. The days of Supreme Court nominations being virtually unanimous are gone, as the chart below makes painfully clear.

Nominee	Nominated	Vote	Passed
Biden			
Jackson, Ketanji Brown	28-Feb-22	53-47	7-Apr-22
Trump			
Barrett, Amy Coney	29-Sep-20	52-48	26-Oct-20
Kavanaugh, Brett	10-Jul-18	50-48	6-Oct-18
Gorsuch, Neil M.	1-Feb-17	54-45	7-Apr-17
Obama			
Kagan, Elena	10-May-10	63-37	5-Aug-10
Sotomayor, Sonia	1-Jun-09	68-31	6-Aug-09
Bush			
Alito, Samuel A., Jr.	10-Nov-05	58-42	31-Jan-06
Roberts, John G., Jr.	6-Sep-05	78-22	29-Sep-05
Clinton			
Breyer, Stephen G.	17-May-94	87-9	29-Jul-94
Ginsburg, Ruth Bader	22-Jun-93	96-3	3-Aug-93
Bush			
Thomas, Clarence	8-Jul-91	52-48	15-Oct-91
Souter, David H.	25-Jul-90	90-9	2-Oct-90
Reagan			
Kennedy, Anthony M.	30-Nov-87	97-0	3-Feb-88
Bork, Robert H.	7-Jul-87	42-58	23-Oct-87
Scalia, Antonin	24-Jun-86	98-0	17-Sep-86

Rehnquist, William H.	20-Jun-86	65-33	17-Sep-86
O'Connor, Sandra Day	19-Aug-81	99-0	21-Sep-81
Ford			
Stevens, John Paul	28-Nov-75	98-0	17-Dec-75

Can you imagine Justice Antonin Scalia being a unanimous selection today? It is also interesting to note the number of justices who did not turn out to be the reliable justice their nominating president (or the Senate) would have thought. This helps underscore the court's independence.

The Electoral College

The Electoral College works, there is a reason for its existence, and it's not going away.

Most of the complaints about the Electoral College begin with the fact that it's not a simple popular vote. But the Electoral College mirrors our country. We are not a pure democracy. We are federal democratic republic. The Constitution vests considerable power and authority with each individual state. It is also why we have a Senate with two senators from each state to balance a House of Representatives that is based on population of each state.

Let me describe the Electoral College a bit more before summarizing my case.

HISTORY

The Electoral College was established in the Constitution's Article II Section 1, Clause 2. Each state is entitled to appoint its own electors in the manner seen fit by their legislatures. The number of electors must equal the total number of the state's congressional delegation. That means two U.S. senators plus each state's number of representatives in the House of Representatives. James Madison defended the Electoral College in "Federalist No. 39" of *The Federalist Papers* as a combination of state-based and population-based government and further argued in "Federalist No. 10" that the Electoral College prevents "an interest and overbearing majority" from commanding undue influence on the selection of the president.

TODAY

Each state has laws that determine how electors are selected and rules they abide by. All but two of the fifty states allow each political party to submit a slate of electors for voters to choose in coordination with their candidates for president and vice president. That means each state's Republican Party selects a slate of electors, and the Democratic Party selects a different slate of electors. The winner of the state's election for president determines which slate is selected to cast their vote. Maine and Nebraska are the only states that do not use this method of selection. Instead, the winner in each of their congressional districts is awarded one elector, and the winner of the statewide vote is awarded two electors. The Electoral College never convenes in one place. Rather, each state's slate meets in their capitals to formalize their votes and then submit them to the U.S. archivist.

WHY DOES IT MAKE SENSE?

Critics often cite recent elections such as 2016 and 2000 as examples of the will of the people being overturned by the Electoral College because the winning candidates lost the popular vote. Moreover, opponents feel the Electoral College violates the principle of one person/one vote. Because there are the same number of electors as there are representatives and senators, the Electoral College deftly balances the interests of the states and the national government. This prevents sectionalism, as Madison argued, and protects the interests of smaller states from being dominated by larger states. The Electoral College ensures the views and beliefs of these smaller and midsize states are accurately reflected and represented. It also compels candidates of both political parties to campaign in those states.

WHY IT WON'T GO AWAY

To remove the Electoral College would require amending the U.S. Constitution. This is a complex process requiring either the support of two-thirds of state legislatures or two-thirds of both the U.S. Senate and the U.S. House of Representatives to convene a constitutional convention to even consider it. Small and midsize states would have no incentive or reason to abolish the Electoral College, as it supports their interests. It would be the same reasoning why these states enjoy having two senators—the same number as the most populous states in the country.

Appendix

General Government

HOUSE: 435 members, as set by 1929 Reapportionment Act.

ROLE: Lower chamber, population based, meant to be more representative of the people. While the House and Senate share "the power of the purse," only the House may originate revenue and appropriation bills, giving them superior control. Other powers shared with the Senate include regulating foreign/interstate commerce, coining money, declaring war, raising an army, admitting new states to the union, and general oversight. Oversight evolved into an incredibly broad power with jurisdiction over almost anything the Congress wants (executive branch, judicial branch, business, entertainment; this ranges from the GameStop hearing to Mnuchin testimony on the annual financial report to Howard Hughes, etc.).

SENATE: 100 members; fixed at two per state.

ROLE: Upper chamber, state-based representation, meant to be more patrician and to serve as a guardrail against the tyranny of a mob majority. Prior to the Seventeenth Amendment's passage in 1913, senators were elected by state legislatures rather than directly by the people, further evidence of this patrician design. The Senate has sole discretion over the confirmation of judicial and executive branch appointments, giving them superior power over federal personnel decisions. Prolonged debate is a hallmark of the Senate. Prior to 1917, there was no limit on debate in the Senate. The Senate Rule 22 adopted that year created the cloture where a two-thirds vote may end debate. In 1975, the cloture threshold was reduced from two-thirds (67 votes) to three-fifths (60 votes).

- Senators receive larger office budgets from $3 million to $4.5 million.
- There are different leadership structures. The Speaker of the House is seen as more powerful than the majority leader of the Senate. This power disparity is reflected in the presidential succession with the Speaker being second in line after the vice president (the majority leader is not listed). The Speaker has almost autocratic control of the House schedule, whereas the majority leader needs more support from the minority leader (not so much recently due to filibuster changes by Harry Reid and Mitch McConnell).
- Senators are generally viewed as more powerful than the average member of Congress. They are 1/100 whereas Members of Congress are 1/435.

- Senators represent entire states compared to the usually smaller House districts.
- House members are elected every two years; senators are elected every six years.
- Age Requirements: House members must be at least twenty-five years of age and citizens for seven years; senators must be at least thirty years of age and citizens for nine years.
- House members are expected to directly represent popular opinion, whereas senators are expected to be somewhat insulated to carefully assess and debate issues.
- The House has the ability to impeach officials, and the Senate must convict them by a two-thirds majority.
- The Senate retains sole authority to ratify treaties by two-thirds majority.

Background on Districts

The Constitution's Article I, Section 2, Clause 3 established U.S. House of Representatives districts based on state population. Their apportionment is determined by the U.S. Census conducted every ten years. Throughout the nineteenth century, the size of the House fluctuated based on census results and apportionment bills passed by Congress. In the early twentieth century, immigration and population shifts dramatically impacted the size of districts. In 1920, Congress did not reapportion the districts due to political power dynamics and the physical limitations of seats available in the chamber. Thus, the last apportionment bill of 1913 stood as precedent capping the total number of districts at 435. Throughout the 1920s, there was unequal district representation with some districts twice the size of others. The Reapportionment Act of 1929 formally capped the number at 435 districts, and it did not extend the previous precedent that districts be contiguous, compact, and equal in populations. Without these requirements, state legislatures greatly expanded their influence over redistricting. Due to partisanship, the parties in control of the state legislatures expanded gerrymandering. With the exception of two terms, the Democratic Party controlled the House from 1931-1994. Moreover due to the 1929 cap of 435 districts, the average population size of districts steadily increased over time while simultaneously seats shifted among the states. Currently, each district represents an average 711,000 citizens with the largest district being Montana at almost 1,000,000 citizens and the smallest being Rhode Island at about 500,000 citizens.

OH-8 History

Ohio's eighth district was created in 1823, just two decades after Ohio officially became a state and during a time of expansive population growth, as people left the East Coast for new economic opportunities. Originally, the Eighth District encompassed central Ohio, including the capital city of Columbus. After the Civil War, the district covered the northern coast of Ohio along Lake Erie. It continued to move around central Ohio until 1970, when it began to cover southwest Ohio. Around this time, Ohio's congressional delegation peaked at twenty-four total districts due to a strong economy and population growth. Ever since, Ohio has lost seats every ten years and is now down to sixteen. The population is largely considered urban (~78 percent) due to residential development outside of major cities such as Cincinnati and Dayton.

House of Representatives

SALARY: $174,00 for a member; the Speaker receives $223,500.

PENSION: Eligibility requirements of at least five years of service; cannot draw until age sixty-two (unless you complete twenty years then you may draw at age fifty or at any age after twenty-five years of service). The formula is complex and contingent on the age of retirement, length of service, and salary. The pension value may be up to 80 percent of the member's final salary or about $139,200 per year. As federal employees, members of Congress can also enroll in the Thrift Savings Plans (TSP), which is comparable to a 401(k). Taxpayer funds are used to match contributions up to 5 percent with an additional 1 percent regardless of employee contributions. Prior to 1942, members of Congress did not receive a pension.

OFFICE: Each member receives an office in one of the House office buildings (Rayburn, Cannon, and Longworth). If they serve in committee leadership, they may also have an office connected to the committee, or if they serve in House leadership, they may also have an office in the Capitol. For instance, Speaker Boehner had his personal office at 1011 Longworth with about twelve staffers then the Speaker's Office in the Capitol with hundreds of staffers.

STAFF: Typically, a member has about twelve staff members in Washington and another ten or so in district offices back home.

BUDGET: Average of $1.38 million per year. If you are in the leadership of a committee, you will be able to draw on the committee budget and staff.

PERKS: Members get to act like the CEO in each office. They set all policies and procedures (causing recent complaints about no uniform HR policies in the House). Members decide budget allocations at will. If they want to pay their chief of staff $10,000/year and their scheduler $150,000/year they may do so, as long as it falls within their allocation. There is lax oversight of the allocations (see former Congressman Aaron Schock's *Downton Abbey* office decoration/mileage reimbursement scandal[31]). Depending on committee assignment, you may get access to "Congressional delegation" trips to foreign countries with staff (often criticized as paid vacations).[32]

TYPICAL COMMITTEE ASSIGNMENTS: Members typically serve on two committees and four subcommittees. Committee assignments are decided by House leadership with a heavy emphasis on seniority (they are also used as political capital to reward loyal allies and punish opponents). Members may serve on a committee for more than ten years before reaching a leadership position.

TIME SPENT HOME VS. DC: Assuming 261 work days, Congress typically spends 55 percent of their time in session in nonelection years and 45 percent of their time in session during election years (2017 and 2018 figures). Members argue they are "always working," especially at home in the district where political responsibilities are significant due to elections every two years.

SIZE OF DISTRICT: Approximately 711,000 citizens per district, with a significant range as noted elsewhere in this book. Geographic size ranges based on population density. Some districts like OH-3 (Columbus) are geographically small with compact populations. Others like OH-6 (southeastern Ohio) span almost 200 miles with rural populations. The entire state of Wyoming is a congressional district.

Endnotes

1   Steven Perlberg, "Rick Santelli Started The Tea Party With A Rant Exactly 5 Years Ago Today—Here's How He Feels About It Now," Business Insider, February 19, 2014, https://www.businessinsider.com/rick-santelli-tea-party-rant-2014-2.

2   In 2012, Mitt Romney won 62 percent.

3   "Congressional District 8, OH," Data USA, accessed April 4, 2022, https://datausa.io/profile/geo/congressional-district-8-oh.

4   John Boehner, "About John Boehner," accessed April 4, 2022, https://www.johnboehner.com/about-john-boehner/.

5   Cristina Marcos and Scott Wong, "Boehner's Top 10 Moments in Congress," *The Hill*, October 29, 2015, https://thehill.com/homenews/house/258497-boehners-top-10-moments-in-congress/.

6   David Nir, "Daily Kos Elections' presidential results by congressional district for 2020. 2016, and 2012," Daily Kos, November 19, 2020, https://www.dailykos.com/stories/2020/11/19/1163009/-Daily-Kos-Elections-presidential-results-by-congressional-district-for-2020-2016-and-2012.

7   Federal Election Commission, *FEC Form 2*, accessed April 4, 2022, https://www.fec.gov/documents/121/fecfrm2sf.pdf.

8   Federal Election Commission, *FEC Form 1,* accessed April 4, 2022, https://www.fec.gov/documents/116/fecfrm1sf.pdf.

9   Federal Election Commission, "Types of nonconnected PACs," accessed April 4, 2022, https://www.fec.gov/help-candidates-and-committees/registering-pac/types-nonconnected-pacs/.

10 American Israel Public Affairs Committee, "About Us," accessed April 4, 2022, https://www.aipac.org/about.

11 Josh Lederman, "Israel to get $38 billion in military aid, U.S. officials say," PBS NewsHour, September 13, 2016, https://www.pbs.org/newshour/politics/us-officials-israel-get-38-billion-military-aid.

12 Federal Election Commission, "Davidson, Warren," Candidate Profile—Financial Summary, accessed April 4, 2022, https://www.fec.gov/data/candidate/H6OH08315/?cycle=2016.

13 Federal Election Commission, "Derickson for Congress," Committee Profile—Financial Summary, accessed April 4, 2022, https://www.fec.gov/data/committee/C00589333/.

14 Deirdre Shesgreen, "Boehner seat candidate: I'll supply concrete for the border wall," *USA Today,* February 1, 2016, https://www.cincinnati.com/story/news/politics/elections/2016/02/01/ohio-8th-district-candidate-trying-out-trump-trump/79640708/.

15 "Did Money Win?" Open Secrets, accessed April 4, 2022, https://www.opensecrets.org/elections-overview/winning-vs-spending?cycle=2020.

16 Warren Davidson (@WarrenDavidson), "This has been done before. #DoNotComply," Twitter, January 12, 2022, 4:47 a.m., https://twitter.com/WarrenDavidson/status/1481216313196437504.

17 Georgia Lyon, "CLC Complains Target Seven Members Who Failed to Disclose Stock Trades," Campaign Legal Center, September 22, 2021, https://campaignlegal.org/update/clc-complaints-target-seven-members-who-failed-disclose-stock-trades

18 Soo Rin Kim, "The Price of Winning Just Got Higher, Especially in the Senate," November 9, 2016, https://www.opensecrets.org/news/2016/11/the-price-of-winning-just-got-higher-especially-in-the-senate/.

19 Daniel I. Weiner, "Fixing the FEC: An Agenda for Reform," Brennan Center for Justice, April 30, 2019, https://www.brennancenter.org/our-work/policy-solutions/fixing-fec-agenda-reform.

20 Open Primaries, accessed April 4, 2022, https://www.openprimaries.org/.

21 FairVote, accessed April 4, 2022, https://www.fairvote.org/.

22 By M.boli—Own work. Derived from an image by Steven nAss, CC BY-SA 4.0, https://commons.wikimedia.org/w/index.php?curid=64401739. Illustration and text altered to adjust for black-and-white color.

23 Pew Research Center, "However You Measure It, Voter Turnover Jumped in 2020," June 10, 2016, downloaded March 28, 2022, https://www.pewresearch. org/fact-tank/2021/01/28/turnout-soared-in-2020-as-nearly-two-thirds-of-eligible-u-s-voters-cast-ballots-for-president/. Pew Research Center bears no responsibility for the analyses or interpretations of the data presented here. The opinions expressed herein, including any implications for policy, are those of the author and not of Pew Research Center.

24 Pew Research Center, "After a Long Decline, Primary Turnout Rebounds," June 10, 2016, downloaded March 28, 2022, https://www.pewresearch.org/ fact-tank/2016/06/10/turnout-was-high-in-the-2016-primary-season-but-just-short-of-2008-record/. Pew Research Center bears no responsibility for the analyses or interpretations of the data presented here. The opinions expressed herein, including any implications for policy, are those of the author and not of Pew Research Center.

25 All data was retrieved from statista.com.

26 Organization for Economic Co-operation and Development, accessed April 4, 2022, https://www.oecd.org/.

27 "Summary of the Byrd Rule," U.S. House of Representatives Committee on Rules, accessed April 4, 2022, https://archives-democrats-rules.house.gov/ archives/byrd_rule.htm.

28 "About Filibusters and Cloture—Historical Overview," United States Senate, accessed April 4 2022, https://www.senate.gov/about/powers-procedures/ filibusters-cloture/overview.htm.

29 JM Reiger, "39 Senators Who Now Support Changing or Eliminating the Filibuster Previously Opposed Doing So," *Washington Post,* June 18, 2021, https://www.washingtonpost.com/politics/2021/06/18/39-senators-who-now-support-changing-or-eliminating-filibuster-previously-opposed-doing-so/.

30 "Chief Justice Roberts Statement—Nomination Process," United States Courts, accessed April 4, 2022, https://www.uscourts.gov/educational-resources/edu-cational-activities/chief-justice-roberts-statement-nomination-process#:~:-text=I%20will%20be%20open%20to,not%20to%20pitch%20or%20bat.

31 Matt Zapotosky, "Former Illinois Congressman with 'Downton Abbey' Office Is Indicted," *Washington Post,* November 10, 2016, https://www. washingtonpost.com/news/post-nation/wp/2016/11/10/former-illi-nois-congressmen-with-downton-abbey-office-to-be-indicted-attorney-says/.

32 Congressional Research Service, "Congressional Salaries and Allowances: In Brief," updated November 3, 2021, https://fas.org/sgp/crs/misc/RL30064.pdf.

Acknowledgments

I SPENT A FEW YEARS wrestling with whether to write this book or not. Some of it was whether I had something to say that was worth the paper and ink, and some of it was whether to rehash a time in my life when I lost. I'm not a good loser.

As I spoke to friends about my time running for Congress, I was constantly reminded that the experience of running for public office itself is not all that common. Some had an idea of what goes on in a campaign but most were astonished by the stories I told. I was encouraged even more following the publication of my first book, *Business Bullseye*. Hopefully, this book will allow a brief a look "under the hood" of what goes on and, just maybe, create the right conversations to effect positive change in our elections.

My wife, Tricia, was the main motivator behind finally getting started on the manuscript. She was there through the whole campaign journey and told me often that I had something of interest and value to share. I would never have run for office without her and certainly would not have written this book without her loving encouragement. She is a rock star to me and our family.

I write about my campaign manager, Baylor Myers, in the book. I did not and cannot say enough good things about Baylor. First and foremost, he is a friend to me and Tricia. That will never change, and we are grateful he was brought into our lives. Throughout the campaign, he worked tirelessly with passion and commitment to getting me elected. In some ways, I'm sorry I disappointed him more than myself, but I like to think that if I didn't lose, then he would not have had the experiences with Treasury Secretary Mnuchin and his career today. Oddly, he's never thanked me for losing.

Matt Rees is not in this book, but he definitely was an invaluable part of it. I got Matt involved before I started writing as a consultant of sorts, and he remained my primary sounding board for the layout and flow of the book as well as the primary editor. He asked good questions, made great suggestions, and generally kept me on track throughout the process.

While not obligatory, I want to also thank my publishers. Naren Aryal and his team are consummate professionals that genuinely helped me succeed in getting to print. Carl Cannon was also very helpful both before I started writing and after I was done. His experience in the political world helped me see a place for this book, and his own stories about politics are just as astonishing.

Last, but not least, thank you to the seemingly small but hopefully growing number of people I have met who believe in, as do I, a more perfect union. You are more important to the future of our country than any politician. Don't ever give up. Don't ever back down.